Optional Protocol
The Involvement of Children in Armed Conflicts

A Commentary on the United Nations Convention
on the Rights of the Child

Editors

André Alen, Johan Vande Lanotte, Eugeen Verhellen,
Fiona Ang, Eva Berghmans and Mieke Verheyde

Optional Protocol
The Involvement of Children in
Armed Conflicts

By

Tiny Vandewiele

Lawyer-linguist at the Court of Justice of the European Communities

MARTINUS NIJHOFF PUBLISHERS
LEIDEN • BOSTON
2006

This book is printed on acid-free paper.

A Cataloging-in-Publication record for this book is available from the Library of Congress.

Cite as: T. Vandewiele, "Optional Protocol: The Involvement of Children in Armed Conflicts", in: A. Alen, J. Vande Lanotte, E. Verhellen, F. Ang, E. Berghmans and M. Verheyde (Eds.) *A Commentary on the United Nations Convention on the Rights of the Child* (Martinus Nijhoff Publishers, Leiden, 2006).

ISSN 1574-8626
ISBN 90-04-14730-6

Cover image by Nadia, 1 $^1/_2$ years old

http://www.brill.nl

PRINTED IN THE NETHERLANDS

CONTENTS

LIST OF ABBREVIATIONS

CRC	Convention on the Rights of the Child
CRC Committee	Committee on the Rights of the Child
DDR	Disarmament, Demobilisation and Reintegration
DDRR	Disarmament, Demobilisation, Reintegration and Rehabilitation
EU	European Union
ICC	International Criminal Court
ICCPR	International Covenant on Civil and Political Rights
ICJ	International Court of Justice
ICRC	International Committee of the Red Cross
ILO	International Labour Organization
NGO	Non-governmental Organization
OAS	Organization of American States
UK	United Kingdom
UN	United Nations
UNICEF	United Nations Children's Fund
USA	United States of America
SC	Security Council
VCLT	Vienna Convention on the Law of Treaties
WHO	World Health Organization

AUTHOR BIOGRAPHY

Tiny Vandewiele works as a lawyer-linguist at the Court of Justice of the European Communities. From 15 October 2003 until 1 July 2004, she was employed as a scientific collaborator at the Human Rights Centre, Ghent University, Belgium, where she was involved in the IAP interuniversity and interdisciplinary research project on children's rights ('Human Rights of Children. Evaluation of the emancipatory character of human rights instruments'). She conducted research on the rights of the child in times of armed conflict, on participation rights of children and on children and international criminal law.

Tiny Vandewiele is a Belgian national, born in 1979. She obtained her law degree from Ghent University in 2002. In 2003, she completed specialized studies in environmental law at the same university. During her studies, Tiny spent a year at the University of Paris-X (Nanterre). She also fulfilled a three-month internship at the International Criminal Tribunal for Rwanda (Arusha, Tanzania).

TEXT OF THE OPTIONAL PROTOCOL

Optional Protocol to the Convention on the Rights of the Child on the involvement of children in armed conflicts, General Assembly resolution A/RES/54/263of 25 May 2000, entered into force on 12 February 2002

The States Parties to the present Protocol

Encouraged by the overwhelming support for the Convention on the Rights of the Child, demonstrating the widespread commitment that exists to strive for the promotion and protection of the rights of the child,

Reaffirming that the rights of children require special protection, and calling for continuous improvement of the situation of children without distinction, as well as for their development and education in conditions of peace and security,

Disturbed by the harmful and widespread impact of armed conflict on children and the long-term consequences it has for durable peace, security and development,

Condemning the targeting of children in situations of armed conflict and direct attacks on objects protected under international law,

Protocole facultatif se rapportant à la Convention relative aux droits de l'enfant, concernant l'implication d'enfants dans les conflits armés

Les États Parties au présent Protocole,

Encouragés par l'appui considérable recueilli par la Convention relative aux droits de l'enfant1, qui dénote une volonté générale de promouvoir et de protéger les droits de l'enfant,

Réaffirmant que les droits des enfants doivent être spécialement protégés et demandant à ce que la situation des enfants, sans distinction, soit sans cesse améliorée et qu'ils puissent s'épanouir et être éduqués dans des conditions de paix et de sécurité,

Troublés par les effets préjudiciables et étendus des conflits armés sur les enfants et leurs répercussions à long terme sur le maintien d'une paix, d'une sécurité et d'un développement durables,

Condamnant le fait que des enfants soient pris pour cible dans des situations de conflit armé ainsi que les attaques directes de lieux protégés

including places that generally have a significant presence of children, such as schools and hospitals,

Noting the adoption of the Rome Statute of the International Criminal Court, in particular, the inclusion therein as a war crime, of conscripting or enlisting children under the age of 15 years or using them to participate actively in hostilities in both international and non-international armed conflicts,

Considering therefore that to strengthen further the implementation of rights recognized in the Convention on the Rights of the Child there is a need to increase the protection of children from involvement in armed conflict,

Noting that article 1 of the Convention on the Rights of the Child specifies that, for the purposes of that Convention, a child means every human being below the age of 18 years unless, under the law applicable to the child, majority is attained earlier,

Convinced that an optional protocol to the Convention that raises the age of possible recruitment of persons into armed forces and their participation in hostilities will contribute effectively to the implementation of the principle that the best interests of the child are to be a primary consideration in all actions concerning children,

par le droit international, notamment des endroits où se trouvent généralement de nombreux enfants, comme les écoles et les hôpitaux,

Prenant acte de l'adoption du Statut de Rome de la Cour pénale internationale, qui inclut en particulier parmi les crimes de guerre, dans les conflits armés tant internationaux que non internationaux, le fait de procéder à la conscription ou à l'enrôlement d'enfants de moins de 15 ans dans les forces armées nationales ou de les faire participer activement à des hostilités,

Considérant par conséquent que, pour renforcer davantage les droits reconnus dans la Convention relative aux droits de l'enfant, il importe d'accroître la protection des enfants contre toute implication dans les conflits armés,

Notant que l'article premier de la Convention relative aux droits de l'enfant spécifie que, au sens de la Convention, un enfant s'entend de tout être humain âgé de moins de 18 ans, sauf si la majorité est atteinte plus tôt en vertu de la législation qui lui est applicable,

Convaincus que l'adoption d'un protocole facultatif se rapportant à la Convention qui relèverait l'âge minimum de l'enrôlement éventuel dans les forces armées et de la participation aux hostilités contribuera effectivement à la mise en œuvre du principe selon lequel l'intérêt supérieur de l'enfant doit primer dans toutes les décisions le concernant,

Noting that the twenty-sixth International Conference of the Red Cross and Red Crescent in December 1995 recommended, inter alia, that parties to conflict take every feasible step to ensure that children below the age of 18 years do not take part in hostilities,

Welcoming the unanimous adoption, in June 1999, of International Labour Organization Convention No. 182 on the Prohibition and Immediate Action for the Elimination of the Worst Forms of Child Labour, which prohibits, inter alia, forced or compulsory recruitment of children for use in armed conflict,

Condemning with the gravest concern the recruitment, training and use within and across national borders of children in hostilities by armed groups distinct from the armed forces of a State, and recognizing the responsibility of those who recruit, train and use children in this regard,

Recalling the obligation of each party to an armed conflict to abide by the provisions of international humanitarian law,

Stressing that the present Protocol is without prejudice to the purposes and principles contained in the Charter of the United Nations, including Article 51, and relevant norms of humanitarian law,

Notant que la vingt-sixième Conférence internationale de la Croix-Rouge et du Croissant-Rouge tenue en décembre 1995 a recommandé, notamment, que les parties à un conflit prennent toutes les mesures possibles pour éviter que des enfants de moins de 18 ans ne prennent part aux hostilités,

Se félicitant de l'adoption par consensus, en juin 1999, de la Convention no 182 de l'Organisation internationale du Travail concernant l'interdiction des pires formes de travail des enfants et l'action immédiate en vue de leur élimination, qui interdit l'enrôlement forcé ou obligatoire des enfants en vue de leur utilisation dans des conflits armés,

Condamnant avec une profonde inquiétude l'enrôlement, l'entraînement et l'utilisation—en deçà et au-delà des frontières nationales—d'enfants dans les hostilités par des groupes armés distincts des forces armées d'un État, et reconnaissant la responsabilité des personnes qui recrutent, forment et utilisent des enfants à cet égard,

Rappelant l'obligation pour toute partie à un conflit armé de se conformer aux dispositions du droit international humanitaire,

Soulignant que le présent Protocole est sans préjudice des buts et principes énoncés dans la Charte des Nations Unies, notamment à l'Article 51, et des normes pertinentes du droit humanitaire,

Bearing in mind that conditions of peace and security based on full respect of the purposes and principles contained in the Charter and observance of applicable human rights instruments are indispensable for the full protection of children, in particular during armed conflicts and foreign occupation,

Recognizing the special needs of those children who are particularly vulnerable to recruitment or use in hostilities contrary to the present Protocol owing to their economic or social status or gender,

Mindful of the necessity of taking into consideration the economic, social and political root causes of the involvement of children in armed conflicts,

Convinced of the need to strengthen international cooperation in the implementation of the present Protocol, as well as the physical and psychosocial rehabilitation and social reintegration of children who are victims of armed conflict,

Encouraging the participation of the community and, in particular, children and child victims in the dissemination of informational and educational programmes concerning the implementation of the Protocol,

Have agreed as follows:

Article 1

States Parties shall take all feasible measures to ensure that members of

---

Tenant compte du fait que des conditions de paix et de sécurité fondées sur le respect intégral des buts et principes énoncés dans la Charte et le respect des instruments relatifs aux droits de l'homme applicables sont essentiels à la pleine protection des enfants, en particulier pendant les conflits armés et sous une occupation étrangère,

Conscients des besoins particuliers des enfants qui, en raison de leur situation économique et sociale ou de leur sexe, sont particulièrement vulnérables à l'enrôlement ou à l'utilisation dans des hostilités en violation du présent Protocole,

Conscients également de la nécessité de prendre en considération les causes économiques, sociales et politiques profondes de la participation des enfants aux conflits armés,

Convaincus de la nécessité de renforcer la coopération internationale pour assurer la réadaptation physique et psychologique et la réinsertion sociale des enfants qui sont victimes de conflits armés,

Encourageant la participation des communautés et, en particulier, des enfants et des enfants victimes, à la diffusion de l'information et aux programmes d'éducation concernant l'application du présent Protocole,

Sont convenus de ce qui suit:

Article premier

Les États Parties prennent toutes les mesures possibles pour veiller à ce

their armed forces who have not attained the age of 18 years do not take a direct part in hostilities.

Article 2

States Parties shall ensure that persons who have not attained the age of 18 years are not compulsorily recruited into their armed forces.

Article 3

1. States Parties shall raise in years the minimum age for the voluntary recruitment of persons into their national armed forces from that set out in article 38, paragraph 3, of the Convention on the Rights of the Child, taking account of the principles contained in that article and recognizing that under the Convention persons under the age of 18 years are entitled to special protection.

2. Each State Party shall deposit a binding declaration upon ratification of or accession to the present Protocol that sets forth the minimum age at which it will permit voluntary recruitment into its national armed forces and a description of the safeguards it has adopted to ensure that such recruitment is not forced or coerced.

3. States Parties that permit voluntary recruitment into their national armed forces under the age of 18 years shall maintain safeguards to ensure, as a minimum, that:

que les membres de leurs forces armées qui n'ont pas atteint l'âge de 18 ans ne participent pas directement aux hostilités.

Article 2

Les États Parties veillent à ce que les personnes n'ayant pas atteint l'âge de 18 ans ne fassent pas l'objet d'un enrôlement obligatoire dans leurs forces armées.

Article 3

1. Les États Parties relèvent l'âge minimum de l'engagement volontaire dans leurs forces armées nationales par rapport à celui qui est fixé au paragraphe 3 de l'article 38 de la Convention relative aux droits de l'enfant1, en tenant compte des principes inscrits dans cet article et en reconnaissant qu'en vertu de la Convention les personnes âgées de moins de 18 ans ont droit à une protection spéciale.

2. Chaque État Partie dépose, lors de la ratification du présent Protocole ou de l'adhésion à cet instrument, une déclaration contraignante indiquant l'âge minimum à partir duquel il autorise l'engagement volontaire dans ses forces armées nationales et décrivant les garanties qu'il a prévues pour veiller à ce que cet engagement ne soit pas contracté de force ou sous la contrainte.

3. Les États Parties qui autorisent l'engagement volontaire dans leurs forces armées nationales avant l'âge de 18 ans mettent en place des garanties assurant, au minimum, que:

(a) Such recruitment is genuinely voluntary;

(b) Such recruitment is carried out with the informed consent of the person's parents or legal guardians;

(c) Such persons are fully informed of the duties involved in such military service;

(d) Such persons provide reliable proof of age prior to acceptance into national military service.

4. Each State Party may strengthen its declaration at any time by notification to that effect addressed to the Secretary-General of the United Nations, who shall inform all States Parties. Such notification shall take effect on the date on which it is received by the Secretary-General.

5. The requirement to raise the age in paragraph 1 of the present article does not apply to schools operated by or under the control of the armed forces of the States Parties, in keeping with articles 28 and 29 of the Convention on the Rights of the Child.

Article 4

1. Armed groups that are distinct from the armed forces of a State should not, under any circumstances, recruit or use in hostilities persons under the age of 18 years.

a) Cet engagement soit effectivement volontaire;

b) Cet engagement ait lieu avec le consentement, en connaissance de cause, des parents ou gardiens légaux de l'intéressé;

c) Les personnes engagées soient pleinement informées des devoirs qui s'attachent au service militaire national;

d) Ces personnes fournissent une preuve fiable de leur âge avant d'être admises au service militaire.

4. Tout État Partie peut, à tout moment, renforcer sa déclaration par voie de notification à cet effet adressée au Secrétaire général de l'Organisation des Nations Unies, qui en informe tous les autres États Parties. Cette notification prend effet à la date à laquelle elle est reçue par le Secrétaire général.

5. L'obligation de relever l'âge minimum de l'engagement volontaire visée au paragraphe 1 du présent article ne s'applique pas aux établissements scolaires placés sous l'administration ou le contrôle des forces armées des États Parties, conformément aux articles 28 et 29 de la Convention relative aux droits de l'enfant.

Article 4

1. Les groupes armés qui sont distincts des forces armées d'un État ne devraient en aucune circonstance enrôler ni utiliser dans les hostilités des personnes âgées de moins de 18 ans.

2. States Parties shall take all feasible measures to prevent such recruitment and use, including the adoption of legal measures necessary to prohibit and criminalize such practices.

3. The application of the present article shall not affect the legal status of any party to an armed conflict.

Article 5
Nothing in the present Protocol shall be construed as precluding provisions in the law of a State Party or in international instruments and international humanitarian law that are more conducive to the realization of the rights of the child.

Article 6
1. Each State Party shall take all necessary legal, administrative and other measures to ensure the effective implementation and enforcement of the provisions of the present Protocol within its jurisdiction.

2. States Parties undertake to make the principles and provisions of the present Protocol widely known and promoted by appropriate means, to adults and children alike.

3. States Parties shall take all feasible measures to ensure that persons within their jurisdiction recruited or used in hostilities contrary to the present Protocol are

2. Les États Parties prennent toutes les mesures possibles pour empêcher l'enrôlement et l'utilisation de ces personnes, notamment les mesures d'ordre juridique nécessaires pour interdire et sanctionner pénalement ces pratiques.

3. L'application du présent article est sans effet sur le statut juridique de toute partie à un conflit armé.

Article 5
Aucune des dispositions du présent Protocole ne peut être interprétée comme empêchant l'application de dispositions de la législation d'un État Partie, d'instruments internationaux et du droit international humanitaire plus propices à la réalisation des droits de l'enfant.

Article 6
1. Chaque État Partie prend toutes les mesures—d'ordre juridique, administratif et autre—voulues pour assurer l'application et le respect effectifs des dispositions du présent Protocole dans les limites de sa compétence.

2. Les États Parties s'engagent à faire largement connaître les principes et dispositions du présent Protocole, aux adultes comme aux enfants, à l'aide de moyens appropriés.

3. Les États Parties prennent toutes les mesures possibles pour veiller à ce que les personnes relevant de leur compétence qui sont enrôlées ou utilisées dans des hostilités en violation

demobilized or otherwise released from service. States Parties shall, when necessary, accord to such persons all appropriate assistance for their physical and psychological recovery and their social reintegration.

Article 7

1. States Parties shall cooperate in the implementation of the present Protocol, including in the prevention of any activity contrary thereto and in the rehabilitation and social reintegration of persons who are victims of acts contrary thereto, including through technical cooperation and financial assistance. Such assistance and cooperation will be undertaken in consultation with the States Parties concerned and the relevant inter-national organizations.

2. States Parties in a position to do so shall provide such assistance through existing multilateral, bilateral or other programmes or, inter alia, through a voluntary fund established in accordance with the rules of the General Assembly.

Article 8

1. Each State Party shall, within two years following the entry into force of the present Protocol for that State Party, submit a report to the

du présent Protocole soient démobilisées ou de quelque autre manière libérées des obligations militaires. Si nécessaire, les États Parties accordent à ces personnes toute l'assistance appropriée en vue de leur réadaptation physique et psychologique et de leur réinsertion sociale.

Article 7

1. Les États Parties coopèrent à l'application du présent Protocole, notamment pour la prévention de toute activité contraire à ce dernier et pour la réadaptation et la réinsertion sociale des personnes qui sont victimes d'actes contraires au présent Protocole, y compris par une coopération technique et une assistance financière. Cette assistance et cette coopération se feront en consultation avec les États Parties concernés et les organisations internatio-nales compétentes.

2. Les États Parties qui sont en mesure de le faire fournissent cette assistance par l'entremise des programmes multilatéraux, bilatéraux ou autres déjà en place ou, le cas échéant, dans le cadre d'un fonds de contributions volontaires constitué conformément aux règles établies par l'Assemblée générale.

Article 8

1. Chaque État Partie présente, dans les deux ans à compter de l'entrée en vigueur du présent Protocole à son égard, un rapport au Comité

Committee on the Rights of the Child providing comprehensive information on the measures it has taken to implement the provisions of the Protocol, including the measures taken to implement the provisions on participation and recruitment.

2. Following the submission of the comprehensive report, each State Party shall include in the reports it submits to the Committee on the Rights of the Child, in accordance with article 44 of the Convention, any further information with respect to the implementation of the Protocol. Other States Parties to the Protocol shall submit a report every five years.

3. The Committee on the Rights of the Child may request from States Parties further information relevant to the implementation of the present Protocol.

Article 9

1. The present Protocol is open for signature by any State that is a party to the Convention or has signed it.

2. The present Protocol is subject to ratification and is open to accession by any State. Instruments of ratification or accession shall be deposited with the Secretary-General of the United Nations.

3. The Secretary-General, in his capacity as depositary of the Convention and the Protocol, shall inform all States Parties to the Convention and all States that

des droits de l'enfant contenant des renseignements détaillés sur les mesures qu'il a prises pour donner effet aux dispositions du Protocole, notamment celles concernant la participation et l'enrôlement.

2. Après la présentation de son rapport détaillé, chaque État Partie inclut dans les rapports qu'il présente au Comité des droits de l'enfant, conformément à l'article 44 de la Convention, tout complément d'information concernant l'application du présent Protocole. Les autres États Parties au Protocole présentent un rapport tous les cinq ans.

3. Le Comité des droits de l'enfant peut demander aux États Parties un complément d'information concernant l'application du présent Protocole.

Article 9

1. Le présent Protocole est ouvert à la signature de tout État qui est Partie à la Convention ou qui l'a signée.

2. Le présent Protocole est soumis à la ratification et est ouvert à l'adhésion de tout État. Les instruments de ratification ou d'adhésion sont déposés auprès du Secrétaire général de l'Organisation des Nations Unies.

3. Le Secrétaire général, en sa qualité de dépositaire de la Convention et du Protocole, informe tous les États Parties à la Convention et tous les États qui ont signé la

have signed the Convention of each instrument of declaration pursuant to article 3.

Article 10

1. The present Protocol shall enter into force three months after the deposit of the tenth instrument of ratification or accession.

2. For each State ratifying the present Protocol or acceding to it after its entry into force, the Protocol shall enter into force one month after the date of the deposit of its own instrument of ratification or accession.

Article 11

1. Any State Party may denounce the present Protocol at any time by written notification to the Secretary-General of the United Nations, who shall thereafter inform the other States Parties to the Convention and all States that have signed the Convention. The denunciation shall take effect one year after the date of receipt of the notification by the Secretary-General. If, however, on the expiry of that year the denouncing State Party is engaged in armed conflict, the denunciation shall not take effect before the end of the armed conflict.

2. Such a denunciation shall not have the effect of releasing the State Party from its obligations under the present Protocol in regard to any act that occurs prior to the date on which the denunciation becomes effective.

Convention du dépôt de chaque déclaration en vertu de l'article 3.

Article 10

1. Le présent Protocole entrera en vigueur trois mois après la date de dépôt du dixième instrument de ratification ou d'adhésion.

2. Pour chacun des États qui ratifieront le présent Protocole ou qui y adhéreront après son entrée en vigueur, le Protocole entrera en vigueur un mois après la date du dépôt par cet État de son instrument de ratification ou d'adhésion.

Article 11

1. Tout État Partie peut, à tout moment, dénoncer le présent Protocole par voie de notification écrite adressée au Secrétaire général de l'Organisation des Nations Unies, qui en informera les autres États Parties à la Convention et tous les États qui ont signé la Convention. La dénonciation prendra effet un an après la date à laquelle le Secrétaire général en aura reçu notification. Toutefois, si, à l'expiration de ce délai d'un an, l'État Partie auteur de la dénonciation est engagé dans un conflit armé, celle-ci ne prendra pas effet avant la fin du conflit.

2. Cette dénonciation ne saurait dégager l'État Partie de ses obligations en vertu du présent Protocole à raison de tout acte accompli avant la date à laquelle la dénonciation prend effet, pas plus qu'elle ne compromet

Nor shall such a denunciation prejudice in any way the continued consideration of any matter that is already under consideration by the Committee on the Rights of the Child prior to the date on which the denunciation becomes effective.

Article 12

1. Any State Party may propose an amendment and file it with the Secretary-General of the United Nations. The Secretary-General shall thereupon communicate the proposed amendment to States Parties with a request that they indicate whether they favour a conference of States Parties for the purpose of considering and voting upon the proposals. In the event that, within four months from the date of such communication, at least one third of the States Parties favour such a conference, the Secretary-General shall convene the conference under the auspices of the United Nations. Any amendment adopted by a majority of States Parties present and voting at the conference shall be submitted to the General Assembly of the United Nations for approval.

2. An amendment adopted in accordance with paragraph 1 of the present article shall enter into force when it has been approved by the General Assembly and accepted by a two-thirds majority of States Parties.

en quelque manière que ce soit la poursuite de l'examen de toute question dont le Comité des droits de l'enfant serait saisi avant la date de prise d'effet de la dénonciation.

Article 12

1. Tout État Partie peut proposer un amendement et en déposer le texte auprès du Secrétaire général de l'Organisation des Nations Unies. Celui-ci communique alors la proposition d'amendement aux États Parties, en leur demandant de lui faire savoir s'ils sont favorables à la convocation d'une conférence des États Parties en vue de l'examen de la proposition et de sa mise aux voix. Si, dans les quatre mois qui suivent la date de cette communication, un tiers au moins des États Parties se prononcent en faveur de la convocation d'une telle conférence, le Secrétaire général convoque la Conférence sous les auspices de l'Organisation des Nations Unies. Tout amendement adopté par la majorité des États Parties présents et votants à la conférence est soumis à l'Assemblée générale des Nations Unies pour approbation.

2. Tout amendement adopté conformément aux dispositions du paragraphe 1 du présent article entre en vigueur lorsqu'il a été approuvé par l'Assemblée générale et accepté par une majorité des deux tiers des États Parties.

3. When an amendment enters into force, it shall be binding on those States Parties that have accepted it, other States Parties still being bound by the provisions of the present Protocol and any earlier amendments they have accepted.

Article 13

1. The present Protocol, of which the Arabic, Chinese, English, French, Russian and Spanish texts are equally authentic, shall be deposited in the archives of the United Nations.

2. The Secretary-General of the United Nations shall transmit certified copies of the present Protocol to all States Parties to the Convention and all States that have signed the Convention.

3. Lorsqu'un amendement entre en vigueur, il a force obligatoire pour les États Parties qui l'ont accepté, les autres États Parties demeurant liés par les dispositions du présent Protocole et par tous amendements antérieurs acceptés par eux.

Article 13

1. Le présent Protocole, dont les textes anglais, arabe, chinois, espagnol, français et russe font également foi, sera déposé aux archives de l'Organisation des Nations Unies.

2. Le Secrétaire général de l'Organisation des Nations Unies fera parvenir une copie certifiée conforme du présent Protocole à tous les États Parties à la Convention et à tous les États qui ont signé la Convention.

CHAPTER ONE

INTRODUCTION*

1. Children are increasingly involved in military activities. They are abducted or (compulsorily or voluntarily) recruited into a State's armed forces or into rebel groups. They are participating in hostilities. Reports suggest that there are more than 300 000 child soldiers in the world today. International law contains more and more provisions dealing with the issue, the most recent one[1] being the 2000 Optional Protocol to the Convention on the Rights of the Child on the involvement of children in armed conflicts.[2] The scope of the Child Soldiers Protocol is commented upon in this contribution. A brief comparison is made with related international instruments.

2. Point of departure for the analysis of the provisions of the Optional Protocol is the text of the Protocol itself, interpreted in a textual, contextual, systematic and teleological manner. The authentic English and French versions of the Protocol are consulted. The Preamble is also considered, since it forms part of a treaty's context.[3] In second instance, additional tools and particularly the *travaux préparatoires*[4] are used. Moreover, documents issued by the Committee on the Rights of the Child, such as concluding observations and reporting guidelines relating to the Optional Protocol, are analysed and treated as an 'authoritative interpretation'.[5] Concluding observations adopted following reports submitted under the CRC also contribute to a good understanding of the vision of the Committee on the Rights of the Child on children and armed conflict, and many of these observations seem to be influenced by the content of the Optional Protocol. Other

---

* September 2004.
[1] Exception be made of the Statute of the Special Court for Sierra Leone (*Cf. infra* note 47), that was adopted just three months after the Optional Protocol.
[2] Hereinafter also referred to as 'Child Soldiers Protocol', 'Optional Protocol' or 'Protocol'.
[3] Article 31 of the Vienna Convention on the Law of Treaties (hereinafter referred to as 'VCLT'); M. Nowak, UN Covenant on Civil and Political Rights. CCPR Commentary, (Kehl/Strasbourg/Arlington, Engel, 1993), p. XXIII, No 18.
[4] Article 32 of the VCLT; M. Nowak, *o.c.* (note 3), p. XXIV, No 19.
[5] Pursuant to Article 40(4) of the VCLT—*Cf.* also M. Nowak, *o.c.* (note 3), p. XXIV, No 21.

provisions of international law, notably of international humanitarian law, are consulted as well. Finally, relevant doctrine[6] and international reports are mentioned.

---

[6] *Cf.* Article 38(1)(d) of the Statute of the International Court of Justice (ICJ), pursuant to which 'the teachings of the most highly qualified publicists of the various nations can be a subsidiary means for the determination of the rules of law'.

CHAPTER TWO

COMPARISON WITH RELATED INTERNATIONAL INSTRUMENTS

3. International law relating to child soldiers is of recent origin. It was not until 1977 that the first universal instrument concerning the recruitment and use of children in armed forces and rebel groups was adopted. Those first provisions are found in international humanitarian law and more specifically in the 1977 Additional Protocols to the Geneva Conventions. In 1989, the issue was introduced in international human rights law, in particular in the Articles 38 and 39 of the Convention on the Rights of the Child. International criminal law and international labour law, respectively in the 1998 Rome Statute of the International Criminal Court and the 1999 ILO Convention No 182 on the worst forms of child labour, also deal with child soldiers. Moreover, certain United Nations resolutions and recommendations discuss the issue.

The only binding regional instrument containing provisions on child recruitment and use in armed conflicts is the 1990 African Charter on the Rights and Welfare of the Child. Some other regional initiatives are nevertheless worth mentioning.

The universal 2000 Optional Protocol to the Convention on the Rights of the Child on the involvement of children in armed conflict is generally more protective than the above-mentioned instruments. Their similarities and differences are examined below. The comparison is limited to the material provisions. As far as procedural provisions are concerned, the Optional Protocol will only be compared to the Convention on the Rights of the Child, when the relevant Articles are examined.

1. *Universal Instruments*

4. As far as universal instruments are concerned, the Child Soldiers Protocol is compared to Article 77(2) of the first Additional Protocol to the Geneva Conventions, Article 4(3)(c) of the second Additional Protocol to the Geneva Conventions, Articles 38 and 39 of the Convention on the Rights of the Child, Articles 8(2)(b)(xxvi) and (e)(vii) of the Rome Statute of the International Criminal Court and Article 3 of ILO Convention No 182 on the worst forms

of child labour. Finally, UN Resolutions 1261 (1999), 1314 (2000), 1379 (2001), 1460 (2003) and 1539 (2004) are mentioned.

1.1   *1977 Additional Protocols to the Geneva Conventions*

5. According to the International Committee of the Red Cross (ICRC), international humanitarian law is 'a set of international rules, established by treaty or custom, which are specifically intended to solve humanitarian problems directly arising from international or non-international conflicts. It protects persons and property that are, or may be, affected by an armed conflict and limits the rights of the parties to a conflict to use methods and means of warfare of their choice'.[7] Provisions relating to the treatment of people in times of war are mainly contained in the 1949 Geneva Conventions[8] and the 1977 Additional Protocols to these Conventions. The two Additional Protocols, dealing respectively with international armed conflicts and internal armed conflicts, marked the first time the issue of child soldiers was addressed in an international instrument.

6. The Protocol Additional to the Geneva Conventions of 12 August 1949, and relating to the Protection of Victims of International Armed Conflicts (Protocol I) of 8 June 1977[9] counts more than 150 States Parties. Provisions on child soldiers are contained in Article 77(2).[10]

In the first paragraph, Article 77(2) states that Parties to the conflict shall take all feasible measures in order that children under the age of 15 years

---

[7] International Committee of the Red Cross, *What is International Humanitarian Law? A Fact Sheet*, available at http://www.icrc.org/Web/Eng/siteeng0.nsf/htmlall/57JNXM/$FILE/ What_is_IHL.pdf?OpenElement. *Cf.* also R. Harvey, *Children and armed conflict. A guide to international humanitarian and human rights law*, (Essex, Children and Armed Conflict Unit and International Bureau for Children's Rights, 2003), p. 6.

[8] Convention (I) for the Amelioration of the Condition of the Wounded and Sick in Armed Forces in the Field, Geneva, 12 August 1949; Convention (II) for the Amelioration of the Condition of Wounded, Sick and Shipwrecked Members of Armed Forces at Sea, Geneva, 12 August 1949; Convention (III) relative to the Treatment of Prisoners of War, Geneva, 12 August 1949; Convention (IV) relative to the Protection of Civilian Persons in Time of War, Geneva, 12 August 1949.

[9] Protocol Additional to the Geneva Conventions of 12 August 1949, and relating to the Protection of Victims of International Armed Conflicts (Protocol I), 8 June 1977.

[10] Article 77(2):
'The Parties to the conflict shall take all feasible measures in order that children who have not attained the age of fifteen years do not take a direct part in hostilities and, in particular, shall refrain from recruiting them into their armed forces.
In recruiting among those persons who have attained the age of 15 years but who have not attained the age of eighteen years, the parties to the conflict shall endeavour to give priority to those who are oldest.'

do not take a direct part in hostilities. In particular, they shall refrain from recruiting them into their armed forces.

As is the case in the Optional Protocol to the Convention on the Rights of the Child,[11] the Additional Protocol only concerns 'direct participation in hostilities' and 'feasible measures'. The interpretation problems to which these terms give rise are discussed further (*Cf. infra* No 28–32 and No 34–36), but it is worth mentioning that a commonly accepted definition does not exist.[12] Whereas Article 77(2) targets children under the age of 15 years, the Optional Protocol extends this protection: Article 1 read together with Articles 3(1) and 4 excludes all under-18s from direct participation in hostilities. Both Article 77(2) and the Optional Protocol are directed towards all parties to the conflict, but given the fact that the Additional Protocol relates to international armed conflicts, it mainly targets States. While the Protocols impose an obligation of means[13] on States Parties, the Optional Protocol limits itself to a moral obligation as far as non-governmental armed groups are concerned (*Cf. infra* No 59–61).

Article 77(2) moreover states that Parties to the conflict shall refrain from recruiting under-15s into their armed forces. This is an obligation of result.[14] The term 'recruitment' has given rise to debate, particularly concerning the question whether or not it comprises voluntary recruitment. For the Optional Protocol, this discussion loses its significance (*Cf. infra* No 38). The Optional Protocol contains more protective provisions relating to recruitment. Indeed, as far as compulsory recruitment is concerned, no person under the age of 18 years shall be recruited.[15] For voluntary recruitment, the minimum age is set at 16 years.[16]

The second paragraph of Article 77(2) establishes the 'priority rule'. In recruiting among persons between 15 and 18 years of age, States Parties shall endeavour to give priority to those who are oldest. A minimal additional

---

[11] *Cf.* Article 1.

[12] *Cf.* J. Mermet, 'Protocole facultatif à la Convention relative aux droits de l'enfant concernant l'implication d'enfants dans les conflits armés: quel progrès pour la protection des droits de l'enfant?', *Actualité et droit international*, 2002, p. 2 (concerning 'direct participation').

[13] And not of result. *Cf.* J. Mermet, 'Protocole facultatif à la Convention relative aux droits de l'enfant concernant l'implication d'enfants dans les conflits armés: quel progrès pour la protection des droits de l'enfant?', *l.c.* (note 12), p. 2; N. Arzoumanian and F. Pizzutelli, 'Victimes et bourreaux: questions de responsabilité liées à la problématique des enfants-soldats en Afrique', *International Review of the Red Cross* 85, No 852, 2003, p. 833.

[14] N. Arzoumanian and F. Pizzutelli, 'Victimes et bourreaux: questions de responsabilité liées à la problématique des enfants-soldats en Afrique', *l.c.* (note 13), p. 833.

[15] *Cf.* Article 2.

[16] *Cf.* Article 3(1).

layer of protection for under-18s is thus, following a compromise, provided for.[17] Given the use of the term 'to endeavour', the obligation is not absolute. As regards the Optional Protocol, the rule is only relevant in relation to voluntary recruitment, since compulsory recruitment of under-18s is in any case prohibited. When recruiting among persons between 16 and 18 years, States should take into account the principles contained in Article 38(3) of the CRC.[18] Hence, the priority rule is implicitly integrated into the Optional Protocol (*Cf. infra* No 48).

7. More than 150 States are Party to the Protocol Additional to the Geneva Conventions of 12 August 1949, and relating to the Protection of Victims of Non-International Armed Conflicts (Protocol II) of 8 June 1977.[19] The issue of child soldiers is dealt with in Article 4(3)(c).[20]

Pursuant to this Article, children who have not attained the age of 15 years shall neither be recruited in the armed forces or groups nor allowed to take part in hostilities. Hence, as in Protocol I, 15 years is set as the minimum age. Protocol II thus imposes two obligations of result,[21] thereby offering extensive protection.[22] However, there is no priority rule recommending recruitment among the oldest first.[23]

No children younger than 15 years shall be recruited in the armed forces or armed groups. The reference to 'armed groups' implies that the provision also targets rebel groups.[24] The Optional Protocol sets higher age limits with 16 years as minimum age for voluntary recruitment and 18 years for compulsory recruitment into the armed forces and 18 years for all recruitment into non-governmental groups. States are, as is the case in Protocol

---

[17] G. Van Bueren, *The International Law on the Rights of the Child* (The Hague, Martinus Nijhoff Publishers, 1998), p. 337; *Cf.* also International Committee of the Red Cross, 'Optional Protocol to the Convention on the Rights of the Child concerning the involvement of children in armed conflicts: Position of the International Committee of the Red Cross Geneva, 27 October 1997', *International Review of the Red Cross* 322, 1998, No 5.

[18] Article 3(1).

[19] Protocol Additional to the Geneva Conventions of 12 August 1949, and relating to the Protection of Victims of Non-International Armed Conflicts (Protocol II), 8 June 1977.

[20] Article 4(3)(c):
'Children who have not attained the age of fifteen years shall neither be recruited in the armed forces or groups nor allowed to take part in hostilities.'

[21] N. Arzoumanian and F. Pizzutelli, 'Victimes et bourreaux: questions de responsabilité liées à la problématique des enfants-soldats en Afrique', *l.c.* (note 13), p. 833.

[22] *Cf.* A. Sheppard, 'Child soldiers: Is the optional protocol evidence of an emerging 'straight-18'consensus?', *International Journal of Children's Rights* 8, No 1, 2000, p. 41; N. Arzoumanian and F. Pizzutelli, 'Victimes et bourreaux: questions de responsabilité liées à la problématique des enfants-soldats en Afrique', *l.c.* (note 13), p. 834.

[23] *Cf.* G. Van Bueren, *o.c.* (note 17), p. 337.

[24] *Cf.* R. Harvey, *o.c.* (note 7), p. 11; G. Van Bueren, *o.c.* (note 17), p. 337.

II, under an absolute obligation to respect this. Whereas Article 4(3)(c) also imposes an absolute obligation on armed groups, the Optional Protocol limits itself to a moral obligation (*Cf. infra* No 59–61).

Children under 15 years of age are also not allowed to take part in hostilities. This provision targets direct as well as indirect participation.[25] The Additional Protocol thus offers a wider protection than the Optional Protocol to the CRC.[26] Moreover, the prohibition is absolute,[27] which is also more protective than in the Child Soldiers Protocol (*Cf. infra* No 27 *et seq.*).

8. The Additional Protocols are only applicable when certain conditions are fulfilled. In the case of Protocol I, the existence of an international armed conflict, an occupation or a deliberation must be established. As far as Protocol II is concerned, the criteria for internal armed conflicts must be met. Hence, before the adoption of the Convention on the Rights of the Child, children involved in civil strives not meeting the conditions for the application of Protocol II could only rely on national law or on the minimal protection offered by Article 3 common to the Geneva Conventions.[28]

1.2 *1989 Convention on the Rights of the Child*

9. In 1989, provisions on children in armed conflicts were incorporated into the 1989 Convention on the Rights of the Child (CRC).[29] This international human rights instrument is ratified by all States except the United States and Somalia. A great advantage of the CRC is that it applies in peacetime as well as to all levels of internal and international conflicts.[30] The relevant provisions for this contribution are Articles 38 and 39 of the CRC.

---

[25] P. Boucaud, 'Droit des enfants en droit international—traités régionaux et droit humanitaire', *Revue Trimestrielle des Droits de l'Homme* 1992, p. 464; N. Arzoumanian and F. Pizzutelli, 'Victimes et bourreaux: questions de responsabilité liées à la problématique des enfants-soldats en Afrique', *l.c.* (note 13), p. 834.

[26] D. Helle, 'Optional Protocol on the involvement of children in armed conflict to the Convention on the Rights of the Child', *International Review of the Red Cross* 839, p. 798.

[27] G. Van Bueren, *o.c.* (note 17), p. 334; A. Sheppard, 'Child soldiers: Is the optional protocol evidence of an emerging 'straight-18'consensus?', *l.c.* (note 22), p. 41; N. Arzoumanian and F. Pizzutelli, 'Victimes et bourreaux: questions de responsabilité liées à la problématique des enfants-soldats en Afrique', *l.c.* (note 13), p. 833.

[28] *Cf.* A. Sheppard, 'Child soldiers: Is the optional protocol evidence of an emerging 'straight-18'consensus?', *l.c.* (note 22), p. 41.

[29] Convention on the Rights of the Child, (hereinafter referred to as 'the CRC' or 'the Convention'), G.A. Res. 44/25, annex, 44 UN GAOR Supp. (No 49) at 167, UN Doc. A/44/49 (1989), entered into force September 2, 1990.

[30] *Cf.* R. Harvey, *o.c.* (note 7), p. 27; N. Arzoumanian and F. Pizzutelli, 'Victimes et bourreaux: questions de responsabilité liées à la problématique des enfants-soldats en Afrique', *l.c.* (note 13), p. 834.

10. Article 38 of the CRC does not significantly extend the protection contained in the Additional Protocols and in international humanitarian law in general[31] and even lowers the standards contained in Article 4(3)(c) of the second Additional Protocol to the Geneva Conventions.[32] The Article was the result of a compromise and should be considered as the 'lowest common denominator' at that time.[33] As regards the issue of child soldiers, Articles 38(2) and (3) are particularly relevant. They are inspired by the Additional Protocols to the Geneva Conventions.[34]

Pursuant to Article 38(2), States shall take all feasible measures to ensure that persons who have not attained the age of 15 years do not take a direct part in hostilities.

As is the case in the Optional Protocol, the CRC only addresses direct participation in hostilities. Moreover, in both the Convention and its Protocol, States are only under an obligation of means:[35] they must take all feasible measures. However, the main difference is that, whereas the CRC is focusing on under-15s,[36] the Protocol extends the protection to all under-18s.

Article 38(3) deals with recruitment into the armed forces.

States Parties shall refrain from recruiting any person under the age of 15 years into their armed forces. This is an absolute obligation of result.[37] A number of States attached declarations to the CRC expressing their dis-

---

[31] R. Harvey, *o.c.* (note 7), p. 12; R. Brett, 'Child soldiers: law, politics and practice', *International Journal of Children's Rights* 4, 1996, p. 117.

[32] Protocol II addresses the indirect participation in hostilities as well as non-governmental armed groups. *Cf. inter alia* F. Krill, 'The protection of children in armed conflicts', in: M. Freeman and P. Veerman (eds.), *The ideologies of children's rights*, (Dordrecht, Martinus Nijhoff Publishers, 1992), pp. 352–353; P. Boucaud, 'Droit des enfants en droit international—traités régionaux et droit humanitaire', *l.c.* (note 25), p. 464; G. Van Bueren, *o.c.* (note 17), pp. 335–338; A. Sheppard, 'Child soldiers: Is the optional protocol evidence of an emerging 'straight-18'consensus?', *l.c.* (note 22), p. 43; R. Brett, 'Child soldiers: law, politics and practice', *l.c.* (note 31), p. 117; M. Happold, 'The Optional Protocol to the Convention on the Rights of the Child on the involvement of children in armed conflict', in: *Yearbook International Humanitarian Law* (The Hague, Asser, 2000), pp. 228–229; N. Arzoumanian and F. Pizzutelli, 'Victimes et bourreaux: questions de responsabilité liées à la problématique des enfants-soldats en Afrique', *l.c.* (note 13), p. 834.

[33] F. Krill, 'The protection of children in armed conflicts', *l.c.* (note 32), p. 355.

[34] *Cf.* N. Arzoumanian and F. Pizzutelli, 'Victimes et bourreaux: questions de responsabilité liées à la problématique des enfants-soldats en Afrique', *l.c.* (note 13), p. 834.

[35] *Ibid.*

[36] These are the only provisions of the CRC which do not apply to all children under 18 years: *Cf.* R. Harvey, *o.c.* (note 7), p. 12; R. Brett, 'Child soldiers: law, politics and practice', *l.c.* (note 31), p. 117. This can be explained by the resistance of States, and more particularly the USA, to change their practice of recruiting and deploying under-18s: *Cf.* R. Harvey, *o.c.* (note 7), p. 27.

[37] N. Arzoumanian and F. Pizzutelli, 'Victimes et bourreaux: questions de responsabilité liées à la problématique des enfants-soldats en Afrique', *l.c.* (note 13), p. 834.

agreement with the low age limit in Article 38.[38] As was already mentioned, the Optional Protocol to the CRC sets the minimum age for voluntary recruitment at 16 and for compulsory recruitment at 18 years and is thus more protective.

Article 38(3) also introduces the 'priority rule' in human rights law. In recruiting among persons between 15 and 18 years of age, States shall endeavour to give priority to those who are oldest. This rule is implicitly integrated into the Optional Protocol (*Cf. infra* No 48).

Contrary to the Optional Protocol, the CRC does not address the issue of recruitment by non-governmental armed groups.[39]

11. Article 39 of the CRC relates to the recovery and reintegration of child victims of several forms of abuse. One of the situations mentioned is armed conflict.

States Parties are under the obligation to take all appropriate measures to promote physical and psychological recovery and social reintegration of a child victim of armed conflicts. Such recovery and reintegration must take place in an environment which fosters the health, self-respect and dignity of the child. A more elaborated provision can be found in Article 6(3) of the Optional Protocol, that focuses on the demobilisation and recovery of child soldiers. The CRC does not contain any explicit provision on demobilisation.[40] The Optional Protocol however seems to impose a weaker obligation on States Parties, since it determines that States Parties shall, when necessary, accord all appropriate assistance. Article 6 of the Protocol also does not contain any reference to the health, self-respect and dignity of the child.

1.3   *1998 Rome Statute of the International Criminal Court*

12. The issue of child soldiers is also addressed in international criminal law and more particularly in the Rome Statute of the International Criminal Court, which counts more than 90 States Parties.[41] The international criminal responsibility of certain recruiters or users is thus established.

---

[38] *Cf.* G. Van Bueren, *o.c.* (note 17), p. 338; M. Happold, 'The Optional Protocol to the Convention on the Rights of the Child on the involvement of children in armed conflict', *l.c.* (note 32), p. 229.

[39] *Cf.* R. Harvey, *o.c.* (note 7), p. 27.

[40] An obligation to demobilise child soldiers could eventually be derived from Article 38: *Cf.* the contribution of Fiona Ang to this Commentary on the Convention on the Rights of the Child.

[41] The Rome Statute of the International Criminal Court, UN Doc. A/CONF.183/9 (1998), entered into force July 1, 2002.

The following is considered a war crime under the Rome Statute: 'conscripting or enlisting children under the age of fifteen years into the national armed forces or using them to participate actively in hostilities' for international armed conflicts[42] and 'conscripting or enlisting children under the age of fifteen years into armed forces or groups or using them to participate actively in hostilities' for non-international armed conflicts.[43]

In international criminal law, the age-threshold is thus 15 years, the Optional Protocol being more protective.

As regards international conflicts, only the national armed forces are mentioned. For internal conflicts, both the armed forces and armed groups are targeted. This is also the case in the Optional Protocol.

For both international and internal conflicts, the terms 'conscription or enlistment' have been used instead of 'recruitment'.[44] Moreover, reference is made to 'use to participate actively in hostilities'. This seems to be broader than 'direct' participation.[45] Indeed, according to the *travaux préparatoires*, the Statute covers both direct participation in combat and active participation in military activities linked to combat such as scouting, spying,

---

[42] Article 8(2)(b)(xxvi).
The Elements of Crime (UN Doc. PCNICC/2000/1/Add.2 (2000)) are the following:
1. The perpetrator conscripted one or more persons into the national armed forces or used one or more persons to participate actively in hostilities.
2. Such persons were under the age of 15 years.
3. The perpetrator knew or should have known that such person or persons were under the age of 15 years.
4. The conduct took place in the context of and was associated with an international armed conflict.
5. The perpetrator was aware of factual circumstances that established the existence of an armed conflict.
[43] Article 8(2)(e)(vii).
The Elements of Crime (UN Doc. PCNICC/2000/1/Add.2 (2000)) are the following:
1. The perpetrator conscripted or enlisted one or more persons into an armed force or group or used one or more persons to participate actively in hostilities
2. Such person or persons were under the age of 15 years.
3. The perpetrator knew or should have known that such person or persons were under the age of 15 years.
4. The conduct took place in the context of and was associated with an armed conflict not of an international character.
5. The perpetrator was aware of factual circumstances that established the existence of an armed conflict.
[44] *Cf.* N. Arzoumanian and F. Pizzutelli, 'Victimes et bourreaux: questions de responsabilité liées à la problématique des enfants-soldats en Afrique', *l.c.* (note 13), p. 839.
[45] *Cf.* D. Helle, 'Optional Protocol on the involvement of children in armed conflict to the Convention on the Rights of the Child', *l.c.* (note 26), p. 3; N. Arzoumanian and F. Pizzutelli, 'Victimes et bourreaux: questions de responsabilité liées à la problématique des enfants-soldats en Afrique', *l.c.* (note 13), p. 839.

sabotage and the use of children as decoys, couriers or at military check-points and the use of children in a direct support function such as acting as bearers to take supplies to the front line, and all activities at the front line itself. Activities manifestly without any relation to hostilities are not covered.[46]

13. The Statute of the mixed Special Court for Sierra Leone reiterates the above-mentioned provisions of the Rome Statute of the International Criminal Court, and contains a provision that can be related to the demobilisation and reintegration of child soldiers.[47]

1.4 1999 ILO Convention No 182 on the Worst Forms of Child Labour

14. International labour law also deals with child soldiers in ILO Convention No 182 on the elimination of the worst forms of child labour[48] and

---

[46] UN Conference Document A/CONF.183/2/Add.1: *Cf.* N. Arzoumanian and F. Pizzutelli, 'Victimes et bourreaux: questions de responsabilité liées à la problématique des enfants-sol-dats en Afrique', *l.c.* (note 13), p. 839.

[47] Statute of the Special Court for Sierra Leone, http://www.sc-sl.org.
Article 4(c):
'The Special Court shall have the power to prosecute persons who committed the fol-lowing serious violations of international humanitarian law:
Conscripting or enlisting children under the age of 15 years into armed forces or groups or using them to participate actively in hostilities.'
Interestingly, in a landmark decision, the appeals panel of the Special Court for Sierra Leone recently ruled that the recruitment or use of children under age 15 in hostilities is a war crime under customary international law. This may result in the first ever conviction for the recruitment of child soldiers. (31 May 2004, Decision on preliminary motion based on lack of jurisdiction (child recruitment). *Prosecutor* v. *Sam Hinga Norman* (Moinina Fofana intervening). Case Number SCSL–2003–14–AR 72 (E).)
Article 7:
'1. The Special Court shall have no jurisdiction over any person who was under the age of 15 at the time of the alleged commission of the crime. Should any person who was at the time of the alleged commission of the crime between 15 and 18 years of age come before the Court, he or she shall be treated with dignity and a sense of worth, taking into account his or her young age and the desirability of promoting his or her reha-bilitation, reintegration into and assumption of a constructive role in society, and in accordance with international human rights standards, in particular the rights of the child.
2. In the disposition of a case against a juvenile offender, the Special Court shall order any of the following: care guidance and supervision orders, community service orders, counselling, foster care, correctional, educational and vocational training programmes, approved schools and, as appropriate, any programmes of disarmament, demobiliza-tion and reintegration or programmes of child protection agencies.'

[48] Convention concerning the Prohibition and Immediate Action for the Elimination of the Worst Forms of Child Labour (ILO No 182), 38 I.L.M. 1207 (1999), entered into force November 19, 2000.

Recommendation 190[49] accompanying the Convention, to which around 150 States are Party.

Forced or compulsory recruitment of children for use in armed conflict is considered one of the worst forms of child labour.[50] Children are all persons under the age of 18.[51] Pursuant to Recommendation 190, States should make such recruitment practices a criminal offence.[52] Convention No 182 is more restrictive than the Optional Protocol where it only targets forced or compulsory recruitment. Moreover, it aims at recruitment 'for use in armed conflict'. Recruitment not directly linked with an armed conflict is thus not one of the worst forms of child labour.[53]

1.5   United Nations Resolutions and Recommendations

15. Besides the mentioned universal treaties, the question of child soldiering has also been addressed by the United Nations Secretary-General and by the Security Council.

16. Within the UN Security Council, support for children's issues has been strengthened considerably.[54] Five resolutions were adopted on child soldiers, the most recent one dating from April 2004. Although not legally binding on States in themselves, those resolutions provide a framework of standards, contributing to the protection of children in armed conflicts,[55] and introducing an additional monitoring mechanism of obligations relat-

---

[49] ILO, Recommendation concerning the prohibition and immediate action for the elimination of the worst forms of child labour, Geneva, 17 June 1999.

[50] Article 3
'For the purposes of this Convention, the term "the worst forms of child labour" comprises:
    (a) all forms of slavery or practices similar to slavery, such as the sale and trafficking of children, debt bondage and serfdom and forced or compulsory labour, including forced or compulsory recruitment of children for use in armed conflict.'

[51] Article 2
'For the purposes of this Convention, the term "child" shall apply to all persons under the age of 18.'

[52] No 12(a).

[53] J. Mermet, 'Protocole facultatif à la Convention relative aux droits de l'enfant concernant l'implication d'enfants dans les conflits armés: quel progrès pour la protection des droits de l'enfant?', l.c. (note 12), p. 3.

[54] Unicef and Coalition to Stop the Use of Child Soldiers, Guide to the Optional Protocol on the involvement of children in armed conflict, (New York, Unicef and Coalition to Stop the Use of Child Soldiers, 2003), http://www.unicef.org, (hereinafter referred to in footnote as 'Unicef, Guide'), p. 9.

[55] R. Harvey, o.c. (note 7), p. 16.

ing to child soldiers. Moreover, UN pressure could be an effective means of implicit implementation and monitoring of the Optional Protocol.

In Resolution 1261 (1999), the Security Council 'strongly condemns' the recruitment and use of children in armed conflict and calls on all parties concerned to put an end to such practices.[56] The Council also urges States and the UN system to facilitate the disarmament, demobilisation, rehabilitation and reintegration of child soldiers.[57]

Resolution 1314 (2000) urges Member States to sign and ratify the Optional Protocol to the Convention on the Rights of the Child.[58] It also requests parties to armed conflict to include, where appropriate, provisions for the protection of children, including the disarmament, demobilisation and reintegration of child combatants, in peace negotiations and in peace agreements and the involvement of children, where possible, in these processes.[59] The special needs of girls should be taken into consideration.[60] These provisions apparently have influenced the concluding observations of the CRC Committee.[61]

Resolution 1379 (2001) reiterates these statements.[62] The resolution is innovative in introducing a new measure in the monitoring process: the Secretary-General should submit a report on the implementation of the resolutions, and attach a list of parties to armed conflict that recruit or use children in violation of their international obligations.[63]

In Resolution 1460 (2003), the Security Council again calls upon all parties to armed conflict to immediately halt recruitment or use in violation of their international obligations.[64] Clear and time-bound action plans to end this practice are to be developed.[65] The Council also calls upon Member States and international organizations to ensure that children affected by

---

[56] UN Security Council Resolution S/RES/1261 (1999), 30 August 1999; No 2; Unicef, Guide, o.c. (note 54), p. 9.

[57] No 15.

[58] UN Security Council Resolution S/RES/1314 (2000) 11 August 2000, No 4; Unicef, Guide, o.c. (note 54), p. 9.

[59] No 11.

[60] Cf. No 13.

[61] Cf. infra on demobilisation and recovery.

[62] UN Security Council Resolution S/RES/1379 (2001) 20 November 2001, Cf. inter alia No 8(c) (girls); No 9(e) (ratification of Optional Protocol and ILO Convention No 182); No 11; No 13.

[63] No 15 and 16. In January 2003, this list was submitted for the first time as an annex to the report of the Secretary General on children and armed conflict. Parties to armed conflict that recruit and use child soldiers had never before been subjected to such a clear denunciation (Cf. Unicef, Guide, o.c. (note 54), p. 9).

[64] UN Security Council Resolution S/RES/1460 (2003), 30 January 2003, No 3.

[65] No 4.

armed conflict are involved in all disarmament, demobilisation and reintegration processes. Hereby, the specific needs and capacities of girls should be taken into consideration, and the duration of these processes should be sufficient for a successful transition to normal life. Particular emphasis is to be placed on education of children demobilized in order to prevent re-recruitment.[66]

In its most recent resolution on children and armed conflict, Resolution 1539 (2004), the Security Council requests the Secretary-General to urgently devise an action plan for a systematic and comprehensive reporting mechanism on child soldiers.[67] Parties in situations of armed conflict on its agenda must prepare within three months concrete time-bound action plans to halt recruitment and use of children. Targeted and graduated measures, through country-specific resolutions, against these parties could otherwise be imposed. The Council reiterates its requests to all parties concerned to continue to ensure that all children associated with armed forces and groups, as well as issues related to children, are systematically included in every disarmament, demobilisation and reintegration process.[68] States and the UN system are called upon to recognize the important role of education in conflict areas in halting and preventing recruitment and re-recruitment of children contrary to the obligations of parties to conflict.[69] The Secretary-General is again requested to submit a report on the implementation of this resolution and the Resolutions 1379 (2001) and 1460 (2003).[70]

In October 1998, the UN Secretary-General established a new policy recommending that all UN Peacekeepers be at least 18 but preferably 21. Civilian police and military observers should be at least 25 years old.[71]

2. Regional Instruments

18. Regional instruments on the rights of the child generally do not address the problem of child soldiers. The only instrument to do so is the African Charter on the Rights and Welfare of the Child. However, some other regional initiatives have been taken.

---

[66] No 13. This also seems to have influenced the concluding observations of the CRC Committee.

[67] UN Security Council Resolution 1539 (2004), S/RES/1539 (2004), 22 April 2004, No 2.

[68] No 8.

[69] No 9.

[70] No 15.

[71] *Cf.* R. Harvey, *o.c.* (note 7), p. 29; Unicef, Guide, *o.c.* (note 54), p. 8.

1.1   Binding Regional Instruments: the African Child Charter

19. The 1990 African Charter on the Rights and Welfare of the Child[72] has more than 30 States Parties. It aims to be complementary to the CRC.[73] Article 22 of the Charter[74] explicitly addresses the issue of child soldiers. Contrary to what could have been expected, the Charter does not contain any provisions similar to those in Article 39 of the CRC and Article 6 of the Optional Protocol (concerning demobilisation and recovery).[75]

According to Article 22(2) of the Charter, States Parties shall take all necessary measures to ensure that no child shall take a direct part in hostilities and refrain, in particular, from recruiting any child. A child is everyone below the age of 18 years.[76]

The Article first contains a provision on 'direct participation'. As is the case in the Optional Protocol, indirect participation is not regulated. Moreover, the Charter and the Protocol target anyone below 18 years. The Charter however is more protective where it asks States to take 'all necessary measures' instead of 'all feasible measures' to ensure this.

Secondly, States shall refrain from recruiting any child. Article 22(2) makes no distinction between voluntary and compulsory recruitment: no under-18 can be recruited into the armed forces. The Optional Protocol is less

---

[72] African Charter on the Rights and Welfare of the Child, OAU Doc. CAB/LEG/24.9/49 (1990), entered into force November 29, 1999, hereinafter referred to as 'African Child Charter'or 'Charter'.

[73] Hence, the Charter should not be considered as an example of cultural relativity: G. Kamchedzera, 'The African Child Charter: Finally in Force amidst Enhanced Justification' in: E. Verhellen (ed.), *Understanding children's rights*, (Ghent, University of Ghent, Children's rights centre, 2001), p. 556; *Cf.* also D. Olowu, 'Protecting children's rights in Africa: A critique of the African Charter on the Rights and Welfare of the Child', *International Journal of Children's Rights* 10, No 2, 2002, p. 128.

[74] 'Article 22
1. States Parties to this Charter shall undertake to respect and ensure respect for rules of international humanitarian law applicable in armed conflicts which affect the child.
2. States Parties to the present Charter shall take all necessary measures to ensure that no child shall take a direct part in hostilities and refrain, in particular, from recruiting any child.
3. States Parties to the present Charter shall, in accordance with their obligations under international humanitarian law, protect the civilian population in armed conflicts and shall take all feasible measures to ensure the protection and care of children who are affected by armed conflicts. Such rules shall also apply to children in situations of internal armed conflicts, tension and strife.'

[75] D. Olowu, 'Protecting children's rights in Africa: A critique of the African Charter on the Rights and Welfare of the Child', *l.c.* (note 73), p. 131; A. Lloyd, 'Evolution of the African Charter on the Rights and Welfare of the Child and the African Committee of Experts: Raising the gauntlet', *International Journal of Children's Rights* 10, No 2, 2002, p. 184.

[76] *Cf.* Article 2.

restrictive where it allows voluntary recruitment as from age 16. However, the Protocol also targets non-governmental armed groups, which is not the case in the Child Charter, although many rebel groups recruit child soldiers.

It can be concluded that the African Charter addresses the issue in a more protective way[77] than the Optional Protocol as far as the armed forces are concerned. This is laudable given the huge amount of child soldiers in the conflict-torn African continent.

2.2   Other Regional Initiatives

20. Regional statements and resolutions concerning the use of children in armed conflict have been adopted. Some of them are mentioned below. They are not binding.

21. Regional conferences resulted in, *inter alia*, the following declarations: for Europe, the 1999 Berlin Declaration on the Use of Children as Soldiers;[78] for Africa, the 1999 Maputo Declaration on the Use of Children as Soldiers;[79] for Latin America and the Caribbean, the 1999 Montevideo Declaration on the Use of Children as Soldiers;[80] for Asia Pacific, the 2000 Kathmandu Declaration on the Use of Children as Soldiers;[81] and for the Middle East and North Africa, the 2001 Amman Declaration on the Use of Children as Soldiers.[82]

22. In America, the Organisation of American States (OAS) adopted the 2000 Resolution on Children and Armed Conflict.[83]

23. In Europe, both the Council of Europe and the European Union have taken some initiatives. The Parliamentary Assembly of the Council of Europe adopted Resolution 1215 (2000).[84] For the European Union, mention can be made of the 1998 Resolution on Child Soldiers of the European Parliament.[85]

---

[77] G. Kamchedzera, 'The African Child Charter: Finally in Force amidst Enhanced Justification', *l.c.* (note 73), p. 558; A. Lloyd, 'Evolution of the African Charter on the Rights and Welfare of the Child and the African Committee of Experts: Raising the gauntlet', *l.c.* (note 75), p. 184; D. M. Chirwa, 'The merits and demerits of the African Charter on the Rights and Welfare of the Child', *International Journal of Children's Rights* 10, No 2, p. 168.

[78] Berlin Declaration on the Use of Children as Soldiers, Berlin, 20 October 1999.

[79] Maputo Declaration on the Use of Children as Soldiers, Maputo, 22 April 1999.

[80] Montevideo Declaration on the Use of Children as Soldiers, Montevideo, 8 July 1999.

[81] Kathmandu Declaration on the Use of Children as Soldiers, Kathmandu, 18 May 2000.

[82] Amman Declaration on the Use of Children as Soldiers, Amman, Jordan, 8–10 April 2001.

[83] OAS Resolution Children and Armed Conflicts, AG/RES.179 (XXX-0/00), 5 June 2000.

[84] Council of Europe Parliamentary Assembly, Resolution 1215 (2000), 7 April 2000, Campaign against the enlistment of child soldiers and their participation in armed conflicts.

[85] European Parliament: Resolution on Child Soldiers, 17 December 1998, Resolution B4–1078.

More importantly, on 8 December 2003 the Council of the European Union adopted the EU Guidelines on Children and Armed Conflict.[86] One of the EU's objectives is to take effective measures to end the use of children in armies and armed groups, and to end impunity.[87] The EU will make demarches and issue public statements urging relevant third countries to take effective measures to end the use of children in armies and armed groups.[88] The Community is engaged in funding projects relating to children and armed conflict in particular for Disarmament, Demobilisation, Reintegration and Rehabilitation (DDRR). Members States will equally seek to reflect priorities set out in the guidelines in their bilateral co-operation projects.[89] These guidelines thus concretise the obligation of international co-operation (*Cf. infra* No 87 *et seq.*) on a regional level.

---

[86] Council of the European Union: EU Guidelines on Children and Armed Conflict, Brussels, 4 December 2003.

[87] No 6.

[88] No 14.

[89] No 15.

CHAPTER THREE

SCOPE OF THE OPTIONAL PROTOCOL

24. The 2000 Optional Protocol to the Convention on the Rights of the Child on the involvement of children in armed conflicts extends the protection provided for by Article 38 of the CRC. Child rights advocates sought for many years to raise the minimum age for recruitment and participation in hostilities from 15 to 18 years.[90] The dissatisfaction with Article 38 also manifested itself within the Committee on the Rights of the Child.[91] At its second session, in 1992, the Committee proposed to draft an Optional Protocol to the CRC in order to further restrict the participation of children in hostilities.[92] It was convinced that this Protocol would contribute effectively to the implementation of the principle that the best interests of the child are to be a primary consideration in all actions concerning children.[93] In 1993, one of the members of the Committee was appointed to prepare a preliminary draft Optional Protocol raising the minimum age of recruitment to 18.[94] Moreover, in the Vienna Convention and Programme of Action adopted on 25 June 1993, the World Conference on Human Rights urged the Committee 'to study the question of raising the minimum age of recruitment into armed forces'.[95] In 1994, the Commission on Human Rights formed an open-ended working group in order to negotiate an Optional Protocol.[96] The working group concluded its work in 2000. The UN General Assembly formally adopted the Optional Protocol on 25 May 2000. After receiving the first 10 ratifications

---

[90] Unicef, Guide, *o.c.* (note 54), p. 7.

[91] Hereinafter also referred to as the 'CRC Committee' or 'the Committee'.

[92] CRC Committee, Day of General Discussion on Children in Armed Conflict (UN Doc. CRC/C/10, 1992).

[93] Paras. 61–77; *Cf.* also CRC Committee, *Concluding Observations:* Germany (UN Doc. CRC/C/Add. 43, 1995), para. 4.

[94] See UN Doc. CRC/C/625, para. 176.

[95] Vienna Declaration, World Conference on Human Rights, Vienna, 14–25 June 1993, UN Doc. A/CONF.157/24 (Part I) at 20 (1993); *Cf.* also M. Happold, 'The Optional Protocol to the Convention on the Rights of the Child on the involvement of children in armed conflict', *l.c.* (note 32), p. 229.

[96] M. Happold, 'The Optional Protocol to the Convention on the Rights of the Child on the involvement of children in armed conflict', *l.c.* (note 32), p. 229.

needed for its entry into force,[97] the Protocol became legally binding on 12 February 2002.[98] As of 4 September 2004, 77 States were party to the Protocol.[99]

25. The Optional Protocol does not entirely meet up to the expectations. Due to the reluctance of some States, in particular the USA, 18 years has not been set as minimum threshold for all recruitment and deployment practices.[100] Indeed, States are still allowed to recruit under-18s when the latter voluntarily join the armed forces. Instead of a 'straight-18' protection, the lowest common denominator has thus been sought.[101] However, it is asserted that the Optional Protocol is 'a significant milestone in the international community's halting journey towards the adoption of a policy that would see the cessation of all forms of recruitment and participation of children in armed conflict'.[102] Its provisions are commented upon below.

Preamble

26. The negotiators of the Optional Protocol easily agreed on the wording of the Preamble.[103] In it, the Optional Protocol is consequently situated within human rights law. International humanitarian law and international human rights law have thus merged with regard to child combatants, with 'human rights considerations infiltrating the body of international humanitarian law'.[104]

---

[97] The first ten States to ratify were the following: Andorra, Austria, Bangladesh, Canada, Democratic Republic of the Congo, Holy See, Iceland, New Zealand, Romania and Sri Lanka.

[98] Unicef, Guide, *o.c.* (note 54), p. 7.

[99] Those States are Afghanistan, Andorra, Argentina, Austria, Azerbaijan, Bangladesh, Belgium, Belize, Bosnia and Herzegovina, Brazil, Bulgaria, Cambodia, Canada, Cape Verde, Chad, Chile, Costa Rica, Croatia, Czech Republic, Democratic Republic of the Congo, Denmark, Dominica, Ecuador, El Salvador, Finland, France, Greece, Guatemala, Holy See, Honduras, Iceland, Ireland, Italy, Jamaica, Japan, Kazakhstan, Kenya, Kyrgyzstan, Lesotho, Lithuania, Luxemburg, The Former Yugoslav Republic of Macedonia, Mali, Malta, Mexico, Republic of Moldova, Monaco, Morocco, Namibia, New Zealand, Norway, Panama, Paraguay, Peru, Philippines, Portugal, Qatar, Romania, Rwanda, Senegal, Serbia and Montenegro, Sierra Leone, Spain, Sri Lanka, Sweden, Switzerland, Syrian Arab Republic, Tajikistan, Timor-Leste, Tunisia, Turkey, Uganda, United Kingdom of Great Britain and Northern Ireland, United States of America, Uruguay, Venezuela and Viet Nam.

[100] R. Harvey, *o.c.* (note 7), p. 13.

[101] A. Sheppard, 'Child soldiers: Is the optional protocol evidence of an emerging 'straight-18'consensus?', *l.c.* (note 22), p. 54.

[102] *Ibid.*, p. 63.

[103] M. Happold, 'The Optional Protocol to the Convention on the Rights of the Child on the involvement of children in armed conflict', *l.c.* (note 32), p. 235.

[104] *Ibid.*, p. 236.

1. Article 1: Direct Participation in Hostilities

27. Article 1 of the Optional Protocol[105] concerns the direct participation of children in hostilities. It determines that States Parties shall take all feasible measures to ensure that members of their armed forces who have not attained the age of 18 years do not take a direct part in hostilities. The fact that only 'direct' participation is targeted is the result of a compromise.[106] The language is drawn from Article 38(2) of the CRC and Article 77(2) of the first Additional Protocol to the Geneva Conventions.

It is worth mentioning that the United Kingdom and Viet Nam made declarations on Article 1. In their view, the Article does not exclude the deployment of under-18s in certain exceptional circumstances.[107]

---

[105] The Committee on the Rights of the Child has adopted reporting guidelines to the Optional Protocol (CRC Committee, *Guidelines regarding initial reports of States Parties to the Optional Protocol to the Convention on the Rights of the Child on the involvement of children in armed conflict* (UN Doc. CRC/OP/AC/1, 2001)). The reporting guidelines for Article 1 determine:

'Please provide information on all measures taken, including of a legislative, administrative or other nature, to ensure that members of the armed forces who have not attained the age of 18 years do not take a direct part in hostilities. In this respect, please provide information notably on:

The meaning of "direct participation" in the legislation and practice of the State concerned;

The measures taken to avoid that a member of the armed forces who has not attained the age of 18 years is deployed or maintained in an area where hostilities are taking place and the obstacles encountered in applying these measures;

When relevant, disaggregated data on members of the armed forces below the age of 18 years who were made prisoners, whereas they did not directly participate in hostilities;'

[106] Unicef, Guide, *o.c.* (note 54), pp. 13–14.

[107] The declarations are the following:

The United Kingdom declared:

"The UK understands that Article 1 would not exclude the deployment of members of its armed forces under the age of 18 to take a direct part in hostilities where:

- there is a genuine military need to deploy their unit or ship to an area in which hostilities are taking place

- by reason of the nature and urgency of the situation

- it is not practicable to withdraw such persons before deployment, or

- to do so would undermine the operational effectiveness of their ship or unit, and thereby put at risk the successful completion of the military mission and/or the safety of the personnel."

In its Concluding Observations relating to the report of the United Kingdom under the CRC, the CRC Committee recommended the United Kingdom to 'take all necessary measures to prevent the deployment of persons below the age of 18 years in the circumstances referred to in the declaration made upon signature by the U.K. of the Optional Protocol, keeping in mind its object and purpose': CRC Committee, *Concluding Observations:* United Kingdom (UN Doc. CRC/C/Add. 188, 2002), para. 54(a).

Viet Nam declared:

"Those who are under the age of 18 shall not be directly involved in military battles unless there is an urgent need for safeguarding national independence, sovereignty, unity and territorial integrity".

1.1   *Direct Participation in Hostilities*

28. The Optional Protocol and its *travaux préparatoires* do not provide guidance on the interpretation of direct 'participation in hostilities' nor do they define the difference between 'direct' and 'indirect' participation.[108]

29. Article 1 of the Protocol refers to the participation of children in 'hostilities' and not in 'armed conflicts',[109] the latter being a broader notion.[110]

In international humanitarian law, references to the notion are more common. At the Diplomatic Conference of Geneva of 1974–1977,[111] 'hostilities' was defined as 'acts of war that by their nature or purpose [strike] at the personnel and *matériel* of enemy armed forces'.[112] During discussions on persons having taken part in hostilities, it was underlined that the term 'hostilities' covers 'not only the time that the civilian actually makes use of a weapon, but also, for example, the time that he is carrying it, as well as situations in which he undertakes hostile acts without using a weapon'.[113] This definition could serve as a basis for interpreting the term under the Optional Protocol.

30. More difficult is the interpretation of 'direct participation' in hostilities. As was already mentioned, neither the Optional Protocol nor the *travaux préparatoires* define the notion.

---

[108] Unicef, Guide, *o.c.* (note 54), pp. 13–14.

[109] *Cf.* International Committee of the Red Cross, 'Optional Protocol to the Convention on the Rights of the Child concerning the involvement of children in armed conflicts: Position of the International Committee of the Red Cross Geneva, 27 October 1997', *l.c.* (note 17), No 42.

[110] Indeed, according to one definition, 'an armed conflict is usually a situation during which there are periods of hostilities, interspersed which periods of truce' (*Cf.* International Committee of the Red Cross, 'Optional Protocol to the Convention on the Rights of the Child concerning the involvement of children in armed conflicts: Position of the International Committee of the Red Cross Geneva, 27 October 1997', *l.c.* (note 17), No 42).

[111] Diplomatic Conference on the Reaffirmation and Development of International Humanitarian Law applicable in Armed Conflicts, Geneva, 1974–1977.

[112] *O.R.* XIV, p. 14, CDDH/III/SR.2, para. 8. *Cf.* also International Committee of the Red Cross, 'Optional Protocol to the Convention on the Rights of the Child concerning the involvement of children in armed conflicts: Position of the International Committee of the Red Cross Geneva, 27 October 1997', *l.c.* (note 17), No 40. Certain delegations considered that the term also covers preparations for combat and return from combat (O.R., XV, p. 330, CDDH/III/224).

[113] Y. Sandoz, C. Swinarski and B. Zimmerman (eds.), *Commentary on the Additional Protocols of 8 June 1977*, (Geneva, ICRC/Martinus Nijhoff Publishers, 1987), hereinafter referred to as 'Commentary on the Additional Protocols', pp. 618–619; *Cf.* also International Committee of the Red Cross, 'Optional Protocol to the Convention on the Rights of the Child concerning the involvement of children in armed conflicts: Position of the International Committee of the Red Cross Geneva, 27 October 1997', *l.c.* (note 17), No 40.

The reporting guidelines of the Committee on the Rights of the Child on the Optional Protocol[114] may provide some guidance.[115] The Committee asks States to specify in their reports the meaning of 'direct participation' in the legislation and practice of the State concerned.[116] Hence, it seems possible to use a more or less broad definition of the term. States are also asked to provide information on 'the measures taken to avoid that a member of the armed forces younger than 18 is deployed or maintained in an area where hostilities are taking place and the obstacles encountered in applying these measures'. It could thus be understood that the mere deployment or maintenance in an area where hostilities are taking place does not amount to 'direct participation in hostilities', but heightens the risk of direct participation.

References to direct participation are also contained in international humanitarian law. According to the Commentary on the Additional Protocols to the Geneva Conventions, 'direct participation in hostilities implies a direct causal relationship between the activity engaged in and the harm done to the enemy at the time and the place where the activity takes place.' In other words, it means 'acts of war which by their nature or purpose are likely to cause actual harm to the personnel and equipment of the enemy armed forces'.[117] Similarly, '[t]here should be a clear distinction between direct participation in hostilities and participation in the war effort. The latter is often required from the population as a whole to various degrees'.[118] According to M. HAPPOLD, taking a direct part in hostilities in essence means 'taking part in combat'.[119]

In its Concluding Observations relating to the report submitted by New Zealand under the Optional Protocol, the Committee on the Rights of the Child asked the State to 'expressly prohibit active service in and outside of New Zealand'.[120] It could be deduced from this recommendation that

---

[114] CRC Committee, *Guidelines regarding initial reports of States Parties to the Optional Protocol to the Convention on the Rights of the Child on the involvement of children in armed conflict* (UN Doc. CRC/OP/AC/1, 2001), hereinafter referred to as 'reporting guidelines'.

[115] *Cf.* reporting guidelines for Article 1 (note 105).

[116] *Ibid.*

[117] Commentary on the Additional Protocols, pp. 516 and 619. *Cf.* also International Committee of the Red Cross, 'Optional Protocol to the Convention on the Rights of the Child concerning the involvement of children in armed conflicts: Position of the International Committee of the Red Cross Geneva, 27 October 1997', *l.c.* (note 17), No 29.

[118] *Ibid.*

[119] M. Happold, 'Child Soldiers', *Netherlands International Law Review*, 2000, p. 36.

[120] CRC Committee, *Concluding Observations: New Zealand* (UN Doc. CRC/C/OPAC/CO/2003/NZL, 2003), para. 5.

legislation of States Parties should be clear about the exact scope of the prohibition: no direct participation is allowed, be it in or outside the country.

31. Are by the majority of scholars considered indirect participatory activities:[121] the gathering and transmission of military information[122] (spying[123] etc.), transmitting orders,[124] the transportation of arms and munitions,[125] the provision of supplies,[126] demining[127] and sabotage.[128] UNICEF on the contrary considers many of these activities to constitute 'direct participation'. In its guide to the Optional Protocol, it interprets direct participation as to 'encompass not only active participation in combat, but also military activities and direct support functions'.[129] These functions might, according to UNICEF, include scouting, spying, sabotage and acting as decoys, couriers, porters, cooks or assistants at military checkpoints. They might also include use of girls for sexual purposes or in forced marriages.[130] This very broad definition is inspired by the Cape Town Principles, that contain a very large, non-legal definition of 'child soldier'.[131] However, it seems improbable that this

---

[121] *Cf.* Commentary on the Additional Protocols, para. 4557 (on Protocol II, Art. 4).

[122] F. Krill, 'The protection of children in armed conflicts', *l.c.* (note 32), p. 353; M. Happold, 'Child Soldiers', *l.c.* (note 119), p. 36; *Cf.* also Commentary on the Additional Protocols, p. 901; D. Helle, 'Optional Protocol on the involvement of children in armed conflict to the Convention on the Rights of the Child', *l.c.* (note 26), p. 2.

[123] A. Sheppard, 'Child soldiers: Is the optional protocol evidence of an emerging 'straight-18'consensus?', *l.c.* (note 22), p. 51.

[124] D. Helle, 'Optional Protocol on the involvement of children in armed conflict to the Convention on the Rights of the Child', *l.c.* (note 26), p. 2.

[125] F. Krill, 'The protection of children in armed conflicts', *l.c.* (note 32), p. 353; M. Happold, 'Child Soldiers', *l.c.* (note 119), p. 36; A. Sheppard, 'Child soldiers: Is the optional protocol evidence of an emerging 'straight-18'consensus?', *l.c.* (note 22), p. 51; D. Helle, 'Optional Protocol on the involvement of children in armed conflict to the Convention on the Rights of the Child', *l.c.* (note 26), p. 2.

[126] F. Krill, 'The protection of children in armed conflicts', *l.c.* (note 32), p. 353; M. Happold, 'Child Soldiers', *l.c.* (note 119), p. 36; A. Sheppard, 'Child soldiers: Is the optional protocol evidence of an emerging 'straight-18'consensus?', *l.c.* (note 22), p. 51; D. Helle, 'Optional Protocol on the involvement of children in armed conflict to the Convention on the Rights of the Child', *l.c.* (note 26), p. 2.

[127] P. Boucaud, 'Droit des enfants en droit international—traités régionaux et droit humanitaire', *l.c.* (note 25), p. 464.

[128] J. Mermet, 'Protocole facultatif à la Convention relative aux droits de l'enfant concernant l'implication d'enfants dans les conflits armés: quel progrès pour la protection des droits de l'enfant ?', *l.c.* (note 12), p. 5; D. Helle, 'Optional Protocol on the involvement of children in armed conflict to the Convention on the Rights of the Child', *l.c.* (note 26), p. 2.

[129] Unicef, Guide, *o.c.* (note 54), pp. 13–14.

[130] *Ibid.*

[131] *Ibid.* The Cape Town Principles were adopted at an international conference on child soldiers held in South Africa in 1997 and have been widely accepted. The definition of 'child soldier' that was adopted reads as follows: A child soldier is 'any person under 18 years of

definition of 'direct participation' will be upheld by the CRC Committee and other relevant actors.

The exclusion of a prohibition on indirect participation is regretted by doctrine and by NGOs, since those kind of activities can be as dangerous as direct participation,[132] and child soldiers are often used in this indirect way.[133]

32. It is clear from the above that the exact definition of 'direct' and 'indirect' participation is uncertain. Hence, it is likely that divergences of interpretation will occur between States and armed groups, thus depriving Article 1 of its meaning.[134] Hopefully, the CRC Committee will provide for a clear and large definition of the notion.

1.2 Members of their Armed Forces Younger than 18 Years

33. Article 1 of the Optional Protocol targets members of the armed forces younger than 18 years.

The notion 'armed forces' has not been defined. According to Article 43(1) of the first Additional Protocol to the Geneva Conventions, 'the armed forces of a Party to a conflict consist of all organized armed forces, groups and units which are under a command responsible to that Party for the conduct or its subordinates, even if that Party is represented by a government or an authority not recognized by an adverse Party'. Contrary to Article 3(1) of the Optional Protocol, Article 1 does not refer to 'national' armed forces. However, a textual interpretation of Article 1—that refers to 'their' armed forces and thus to the States Parties—shows that this Article also targets national armed forces. The armed forces thus are mainly linked to States, usually including a country's army, navy and air force.[135]

---

age who is part of any kind of regular or irregular armed force or armed group in any capacity, including but not limited to cooks, porters, messengers and anyone accompanying such groups, other than family members. The definition includes girls recruited for sexual purposes and forced marriage.' The Cape Town definition is for programmatic purposes and is not a legal definition.

[132] G. Van Bueren, o.c. (note 17), p. 334; M. Happold, 'The Optional Protocol to the Convention on the Rights of the Child on the involvement of children in armed conflict', l.c. (note 32), p. 237.

[133] F. Grünfeld, 'Child soldiers', in J. Willems (ed.), *Developmental and autonomy rights of children. Empowering children, caregivers and communities*, Antwerpen/Oxford/New York, Intersentia, 2002, p. 284.

[134] International Committee of the Red Cross, 'Optional Protocol to the Convention on the Rights of the Child concerning the involvement of children in armed conflicts: Position of the International Committee of the Red Cross Geneva, 27 October 1997', l.c. (note 17), No 30.

[135] *Cf.* several dictionary definitions.

Article 1 should be read together with Articles 2 (no compulsory recruitment of under-18s) and 3 (voluntary recruitment possible between 16 and 18 years). Consequently, the notion 'members of the armed forces younger than 18 years' is to be understood as meaning persons between 16 and 18 years of age that voluntarily joined a country's military forces.

1.3   Obligation of Means Resting on States Parties

34. States Parties shall take all feasible measures to ensure that under-18s do not directly participate in hostilities. How should the notion 'all feasible measures' be interpreted and what measures could States *in concreto* take?

35. The term 'feasible measures' has not been defined.

Firstly, it should be observed that because of the use of the term 'feasible', the obligation to ensure that no under-18 directly participates in hostilities is not absolute.[136] It is an obligation of means[137] or conduct[138] and not an obligation of result. Since under-18s may be recruited into the armed forces, it will not be possible to avoid their direct participation in hostilities at all times.[139] It is sufficient that 'all feasible measures' have been taken in this regard.

References to 'feasible measures' can also be found in international humanitarian law and more specifically in Articles 76(3), 57 and 58 of the first Additional Protocol to the Geneva Conventions. According to the International Committee of the Red Cross (ICRC), the expression is to be understood in its dictionary meaning, 'feasible' then meaning 'capable of being done, accomplished or carried out, possible or practicable'.[140] However, it has been argued that this definition in itself is not clear.[141] Indeed, 'possible' and 'practicable' are distinct notions. Something 'possible' refers to 'whether it can be done at all', whereas something 'practicable' refers to 'whether, in the particular circumstances of the moment, the efforts required to do it

---

[136] M. Happold, 'The Optional Protocol to the Convention on the Rights of the Child on the involvement of children in armed conflict', *l.c.* (note 32), p. 236.

[137] M. Happold, 'Child Soldiers', *l.c.* (note 119), p. 35; M. Happold, 'The Optional Protocol to the Convention on the Rights of the Child on the involvement of children in armed conflict', *l.c.* (note 32), p. 236.

[138] D. Helle, 'Optional Protocol on the involvement of children in armed conflict to the Convention on the Rights of the Child', *l.c.* (note 26), p. 2.

[139] M. Happold, 'The Optional Protocol to the Convention on the Rights of the Child on the involvement of children in armed conflict', *l.c.* (note 32), p. 237.

[140] *Cf.* M. Happold, 'Child Soldiers', *l.c.* (note 119), p. 34.

[141] *Ibid.*

are not disproportionate to the result obtained on having done so'.[142] Moreover, 'whatever is under the jurisdiction and control of a party is *prima facie* capable of being done. It may however not always be feasible to ensure implementation at every level'.[143] The concept of 'feasible' measures also refers to the circumstances in which the measures are to be taken.[144] Hence, some considered 'feasible' to mean 'which is practicable or practically possible taking into account all circumstances ruling at the time, including humanitarian and military considerations'.[145] However, the conclusion seems to be different in relation to the Optional Protocol. The French version of Article 1 refers to 'toutes les mesures possibles'. Contrary to Article 38(2) CRC ('toutes les mesures possibles dans la pratique'), no reference is made to 'practice' or 'practicable'. This seems to imply that the term 'feasible' in the Optional Protocol should be interpreted more broadly than in the Additional Protocols and the CRC, thereby imposing a more stringent obligation on States Parties. The exact interpretation of 'feasible measures' is in any case uncertain. Moreover, the question of what is and what is not 'feasible' in a particular context is likely to be controversial. Indeed, when is it not 'feasible' for a commander to withhold or remove a soldier younger than 18 from direct participation in hostilities?[146] The Committee on the Rights of the Child can play an important role in specifying the notion[147] and the corresponding obligations for States Parties.

36. What measures could States *in concreto* take? The reporting guidelines issued by the Committee on the Rights of the Child give some indications.[148] Measures can be of a legislative, administrative or other nature, and could include measures to avoid that a member of the armed forces who has not attained the age of 18 years is deployed or maintained in an area where hostilities are taking place. No other indication can be deduced from the

---

[142] *Ibid.*

[143] G. Goodwinn-Gill and I. Cohn, *Child Soldiers. The role of children in armed conflicts*, (Oxford, Clarendon Press, 1994), p. 63.

[144] M. Happold, 'Child Soldiers', *l.c.* (note 119), p. 34.

[145] M.J. Dennis, 'The ILO Convention on the worst forms of child labor', *The American Journal of International Law* 93, No 4, 1999, p. 791; M. Happold, 'Child Soldiers', *l.c.* (note 119), p. 35; *Cf.* also Diplomatic Conference on the adoption of Article 57 of the first Additional Protocol to the Geneva Conventions.

[146] M.J. Dennis, 'The ILO Convention on the worst forms of child labor', *l.c.* (note 145), p. 791.

[147] *Cf.* D. Helle, 'Optional Protocol on the involvement of children in armed conflict to the Convention on the Rights of the Child', *l.c.* (note 26), p. 2.

[148] *Cf.* reporting guidelines for Article 1 (note 105).

reporting guidelines. The CRC Committee will thus need to further precise the obligations resting on States Parties. In its concluding observations to reports submitted under the CRC, the Committee already recommended that States Parties should set up a comprehensive strategy to ensure that no children are involved in armed conflict.[149] Preventive measures need to be adopted[150] and measures taken must be effective.[151] Measures implementing Article 1 should be situated within this framework.

2. Article 2: Compulsory recruitment

37. Article 2 of the Optional Protocol[152] concerns the compulsory recruitment of children. States Parties shall ensure that persons who have not attained the age of 18 years are not compulsorily recruited into their armed forces. The prohibition reflects an emerging straight-18–approach,[153] but is not applauded by everyone. Indeed, it is regretted that Article 2 (implicitly) and Article 3 (explicitly) recognize the possibility to voluntarily recruit children. Andorra and Portugal even attached declarations to the Protocol to express their dissatisfaction herewith.

---

[149] CRC Committee, *Concluding Observations:* Papua New Guinea (UN Doc. CRC/C/Add. 229, 2004), para. 56.

[150] CRC Committee, *Concluding Observations:* Indonesia (UN Doc. CRC/C/Add. 223, 2004), para. 71(d).

[151] CRC Committee, *Concluding Observations:* Pakistan (UN Doc. CRC/C/Add. 217, 2003), para. 68.

[152] The reporting guidelines for Article 2 determine:
'Please indicate all the measures taken including of a legislative, administrative or other nature, to ensure that persons who have not attained the age 18 years are not compulsorily recruited into the armed forces. In this regard, reports should indicate among others:
• Detailed information on the process of compulsory recruitment (i.e. from registration up to the physical integration into the armed forces) indicating the minimum age linked to each step and, at what time in that process, recruits become members of the armed forces;
• The reliable documents to verify age, which are required prior to acceptance into compulsory military service (birth certificate, affidavit, *etc.*);
• Any legal provision enabling the age of conscription to be lowered in exceptional circumstances (e.g. state of emergency). In this respect, please provide information on the age it can be lowered to, the process and the conditions for that change.
• For States Parties where compulsory military service has been suspended but not abolished, the minimum age of recruitment set up in the previous regime and how, and under what conditions, this previous system can be reinstalled.'

[153] *Cf.* A. Sheppard, 'Child soldiers: Is the optional protocol evidence of an emerging 'straight-18'consensus ?', *l.c.* (note 22).

2.1 *Compulsory Recruitment into their Armed Forces*

38. 'Compulsory recruitment' is not easy to define.

The ordinary meaning of 'recruit' is 'to strengthen, reinforce or replenish, irrespective of source or method'.[154] According to the Commentary on the Additional Protocols to the Geneva Conventions, recruitment covers 'any means by which a person becomes a member of the armed forces or an armed group'.[155] What counts is the competence to control entry into the armed forces'.[156] Technically, a formal act of recruitment by the organization is required.[157] It can go from a conscription to a general mobilization in times of imminent conflict.[158] Recruitment includes cross-border recruitment.[159] In the past, some scholars considered recruitment to cover compulsory as well as voluntary enrolment in the armed forces,[160] while others limited its meaning to compulsory recruitment.[161] As far as the Optional Protocol is concerned, this discussion loses its significance. Indeed, a clear distinction is made between the rules on compulsory (Article 2) and voluntary (Article 3) recruitment, thereby implying that recruitment can be both compulsory and voluntary.

The interpretation of 'compulsory' is debated as well. The notion usually implies that a certain force makes the person do something.[162] It is thus obvious that the distinction between voluntary and compulsory (*Cf. infra* No 45) recruitment may be difficult to implement in practice, since volunteers might for example be coerced by lack of food, the need for physical protection, poverty or revenge.[163]

---

[154] G. Goodwinn-Gill and I. Cohn, *o.c.* (note 143), p. 62.

[155] Commentary on the Additional Protocols to the Geneva Conventions.

[156] G. Goodwinn-Gill and I. Cohn, *o.c.* (note 143), p. 62.

[157] *Cf.* A. Sheppard, 'Child soldiers: Is the optional protocol evidence of an emerging 'straight-18'consensus?', *l.c.* (note 22), p. 50.

[158] J. Mermet, 'Protocole facultatif à la Convention relative aux droits de l'enfant concernant l'implication d'enfants dans les conflits armés: quel progrès pour la protection des droits de l'enfant?', *l.c.* (note 12), p. 4.

[159] This could *inter alia* be derived from the Preamble ('within and across national borders') and from the recommendations of the Committee on the Rights of the Child in CRC Committee, *Concluding Observations:* Democratic Republic of the Congo (UN Doc. CRC/C/Add. 153, 2001), para. 65.

[160] E.g. M. Dutli, 'Captured child combatants', *International Review of the Red Cross* 278, p. 421 (*Cf.* G. Van Bueren, *o.c.* (note 17), p. 336); G. Goodwinn-Gill and I. Cohn, *o.c.* (note 143), p. 62 note 9.

[161] *Cf.* G. Goodwinn-Gill and I. Cohn, *o.c.* (note 143), p. 62; F. Grünfeld, 'Child soldiers', *l.c.* (note 133), p. 282.

[162] *Cf.* several dictionary definitions.

[163] Unicef, Guide, *o.c.* (note 54), p. 16. *Cf.* also D. Helle, 'Optional Protocol on the involvement of children in armed conflict to the Convention on the Rights of the Child', *l.c.* (note 26), p. 4.

39. The notion 'armed forces' has been analysed above (*Cf. supra* No 33). The reference to 'their' armed forces implies that the national armed forces of a State party are concerned.

2.2   Persons Who Have Not Attained the Age of 18 Years

40. The compulsory recruitment of 'persons who have not attained the age of 18 years' is prohibited. The Optional Protocol thus raises the standards that previously had been set at 15 years by international law.[164] From the day that a person turns 18, he/she can be compulsorily recruited into the armed forces. The anniversary of the person concerned should be taken into consideration as point of departure and not the first of January of the year in which the recruit reaches the age of 18.[165]

It is interesting to note that the Protocol does not refer to 'children' but to 'persons'. According to Article 1 of the CRC, a child means every human being below the age of eighteen years unless under the law applicable to the child, majority is attained earlier. The interdiction of compulsory recruitment imposed by the Optional Protocol thus equally applies to adults younger than 18 years.

2.3   Obligation of Result Resting on States Parties

41. The 'States Parties' shall ensure that no under-18s are compulsorily recruited into their armed forces. Hence, the prohibition of compulsory recruitment does not target the under-18s themselves but the authorities that control the recruitment process.[166]

In contrast to Article 1, the obligation contained in Article 2 is absolute,[167] thus being an obligation of result. A problem raises when States have not established a proper birth registration system, as is often the case in developing countries. According to M. HAPPOLD and the UNICEF guide to the Optional Protocol, in such cases, States should not recruit anyone who might be under the age of 18. If a State even inadvertently does so, it will act in breach of Article 2.[168]

---

[164] Unicef, Guide, *o.c.* (note 54), p. 4 and p. 15; D. Helle, 'Optional Protocol on the involvement of children in armed conflict to the Convention on the Rights of the Child', *l.c.* (note 26), p. 3

[165] J. Mermet, 'Protocole facultatif à la Convention relative aux droits de l'enfant concernant l'implication d'enfants dans les conflits armés: quel progrès pour la protection des droits de l'enfant?', *l.c.* (note 12), p. 4.

[166] *Cf.* G. Goodwinn-Gill and I. Cohn, *o.c.* (note 143), p. 61.

[167] *Cf.* reporting guidelines for Article 2 (note 152).

[168] Unicef, Guide, *o.c.* (note 54), p. 16; M. Happold, 'The Optional Protocol to the Convention

42. No real indications about the measures that States should *in concreto* take, are provided for. According to the reporting guidelines, measures can be of a legislative, administrative or other nature. Reliable documents to verify age, such as birth certificates, affidavits *etc.*, should be asked for. The process of compulsory recruitment, i.e. from the registration up to the physical integration into the armed forces, needs to guarantee that the age requirement is satisfied.

3. *Article 3: Voluntary Recruitment*

43. Article 3 of the Optional Protocol concerns voluntary recruitment into the national armed forces. It consists of 5 paragraphs establishing a framework within which under-18s can be recruited into the armed forces. Article 3 asks States Parties to raise the minimum age for voluntary recruitment to 16 years (or above). States must deposit a binding declaration setting forth this minimum age. That declaration can be strengthened at any time. The article also contains safeguards that need to ensure the protection of adolescents joining the armed forces. Finally, an exemption is made for military schools.

Many participants considered 'voluntary' recruitment of children impossible and were thus in favour of 18 years as minimum age for all recruitment. This straight-18–approach was, and still is, supported by the Committee on the Rights of the Child.[169] Others on the contrary considered that, following a practice in many countries, 17 should be the minimum age for voluntary recruitment.[170] It was also argued that the imposition of an 18–years age limit undermines an important accessory purpose of military service, namely educating young people.[171] Article 3 thus reflects a compromise.

---

on the Rights of the Child on the involvement of children in armed conflict', *l.c.* (note 32), p. 237.

[169] *Cf.* CRC Committee, Day of General Discussion on Children in Armed Conflict (UN Doc. CRC/C/10, 1992); CRC Committee, *Concluding Observations:* Bhutan (UN Doc. CRC/C/Add. 157, 2001), paras. 54 and 55; Paraguay (UN Doc. CRC/C/Add. 166, 2001), para. 46(f); Israel (UN Doc. CRC/C/Add. 195, 2002), para. 59(b); Sudan (UN Doc. CRC/C/Add. 190, 2002, para. 60(a); United Kingdom (UN Doc. CRC/C/Add. 188, 2002), para. 54(b); Canada (UN Doc. CRC/C/Add. 215, 2003), para. 49; New Zealand (UN Doc. CRC/C/OPAC/CO/2003/NZL, 2003), para. 7; Germany (UN Doc. CRC/C/Add.226, 2004), para. 62; Democratic People's Republic of Korea (UN Doc. CRC/C/Add. 239, 2004), para. 57; Liberia (UN Doc. CRC/C/Add. 236, 2004), para. 59(b).

[170] S. Detrick, *A commentary on the United Nations Convention on the Rights of the Child*, (The Hague/Boston/London, Martinus Nijhoff Publishers, 1999), p. 660.

[171] S. Detrick, *o.c.* (note 171), p. 660; *Cf.* also Unicef, Guide, *o.c.* (note 54), p. 16.

3.1   *Article 3(1): Higher Minimum Age*

44. Article 3(1) of the Optional Protocol[172] determines that States shall raise in years the minimum age for the voluntary recruitment of persons into their national armed forces from that set out in Article 38(3) CRC, taking account of the principles contained in that article and recognizing that under the Convention persons under the age of 18 years are entitled to special protection.

45. The debates on the notion of 'recruitment' have been dealt with above (*Cf. supra* No 38). According to UNICEF, 'voluntary' recruitment means that 'children are under no compulsion to join armed forces and that safeguards are in place to ensure that any voluntary recruitment is genuinely voluntary'.[173] As was already mentioned, it remains uncertain how the distinction with compulsory recruitment should be made. In any case, recruitment should not be forced or coerced.[174] Again, the term 'persons' has been used instead of 'children' (*Cf. supra* No 40).

46. The notion 'armed forces' has been examined above. Interestingly, Article 3(1) explicitly refers to 'national' armed forces. However, this does not seem to add something new, since Articles 1, 2 and 3 also target a country's national military forces (*Cf. supra* No 34 and No 40).

47. Article 38(3) of the CRC sets out a minimum age of 15 years for recruitment and direct participation in hostilities (*Cf. supra* No 10). According to the Protocol, States shall raise in years the minimum age from that set out in this Article. The obligation is absolute. Hence, in a rather opaque man-

---

[172] The reporting guidelines for Article 3(1) determine:
'Reports should notably indicate:
• The minimum age set out for voluntary recruitment into the armed forces, in accordance with the declaration submitted upon ratification or accession or any change thereafter;
• When relevant, disaggregated data on children below the age of 18 years voluntarily recruited into the national armed forces (for example, by gender, age, region, rural/urban areas and social and ethnic origin, and military ranks);
• When relevant, pursuant to article 38, paragraph 3 of the Convention on the Rights of the Child, the measures taken to ensure that in recruiting those persons who have attained the minimum age set out for voluntary recruitment but who have not attained the age of 18 years, priority is given to those who are the oldest. In this respect, please provide information on the measures of special protection adopted for the under-18–years-old recruits.'
[173] Unicef, Guide, *o.c.* (note 54), p. 16.
[174] *Cf.* Article 3(2): '[. . .] a description of the safeguards it has adopted to ensure that such recruitment is not *forced or coerced*', emphasis added.

ner, the minimum age for voluntary recruitment has been set at 16 years.[175] This obligation of result is concretized in the obligation to deposit a binding declaration upon ratification or accession setting out the minimum age: without raising that age, a State cannot become Party to the Protocol (*Cf. infra* No 50).

Interestingly, the CRC Committee, in its Concluding Observations relating to the report submitted under the Optional Protocol by New Zealand, recommended that the State Party consider the possibility of increasing the minimum age for voluntary recruitment to 18 years.[176] It thus keeps on supporting its straight-18–position.

48. Article 3(1) states that the 'principles' contained in 'that article' should be taken account of. This requirement includes States that are party to the Optional Protocol but not to the CRC itself. The question raises whether this provision refers to Article 38(3) or to Article 38 of the CRC in its entirety. What principles are contained in that article? The Reporting guidelines provide some guidance in that regard. They ask States to indicate, when relevant, the measures taken to ensure that in recruiting among persons between 16 and 18 years, priority is given to those who are the oldest.[177] It could thus be concluded that the priority rule contained in Article 38(3) of the CRC is implicitly integrated into the Optional Protocol.[178] However, it is unclear what effect the requirement to take these principles into account is meant to have. 'If the provision is not simply hortatory, then it seems only to impose a weak obligation on States to consider whether it is appropriate to recruit under-18 year olds and to set out criteria which they must take into account when making their decision whether to do so. The lack of clarity leads to a suspicion that the provision was a sop to States which wished for a higher standard of protection', says M. HAPPOLD.[179]

49. States need to recognize that under the CRC, under-18s are entitled to special protection. Since the reporting guidelines ask States to provide information on the measures of special protection for recruits below the age of

---

[175] M. Happold, 'The Optional Protocol to the Convention on the Rights of the Child on the involvement of children in armed conflict', *l.c.* (note 32), p. 238.

[176] CRC Committee, *Concluding Observations:* New Zealand (UN Doc. CRC/C/OPAC/CO/2003/NZL, 2003), para. 7.

[177] *Cf.* reporting guidelines for Article 3(1) (note 173).

[178] *Cf.* also CRC Committee, *Concluding Observations:* Canada (UN Doc. CRC/C/Add. 215, 2003), para. 49.

[179] M. Happold, 'The Optional Protocol to the Convention on the Rights of the Child on the involvement of children in armed conflict', *l.c.* (note 32), p. 238.

18, this obligation only seems to target under-age recruits. It could be deduced from the guidelines that States are to take active measures to ensure this protection. The exact scope of the obligation is not clear: are States under an obligation of means or an obligation of result? What is to be understood by 'special protection'? Is this the whole system of protection installed by the CRC or are only 'special' measures targeted? The interpretation of the CRC Committee on the scope of 'recognition' and 'special protection' is thus to be waited for.

3.2   Article 3(2): Binding Declaration

50. Article 3(2) of the Optional Protocol[180] deals with the binding declaration that States Parties need to deposit upon ratification or accession. In this declaration, States must set forth the minimum age at which they will permit voluntary recruitment into their national armed forces and describe the safeguards they have adopted to ensure that such recruitment is not forced or coerced (*Cf. infra* No 52). If States fail to submit a binding declaration, the instrument of ratification or accession will not be accepted in deposit but will be held pending.[181] The Committee on the Rights of the Child will evaluate the declarations setting forth a minimum age below 18 years on their correspondence with the object and goal of the Protocol.[182] The initial declarations can be strengthened at any time (*Cf. infra* No 55). Reports should, according to the reporting guidelines,[183] provide information on the debate that has taken place prior to the adoption of the binding declaration and the people involved in the debate. The Committee is thus interested in the degree and way of reaching consensus in the State concerned on the minimum age.

---

[180] The reporting guidelines for Article 3(2) juncto Article 3(4) determine:
'Reports should notably provide information on:
 • The debate which has taken place in the State concerned prior to the adoption of the binding declaration and the people involved in that debate;
 • When relevant, the national [or regional, local, *etc.*] debates, initiatives or any campaign aiming at strengthening the declaration if it set out a minimum age lower than 18 years.'

[181] Unicef, Guide, *o.c.* (note 54), p. 26.

[182] *Cf.* J. Mermet, 'Protocole facultatif à la Convention relative aux droits de l'enfant concernant l'implication d'enfants dans les conflits armés: quel progrès pour la protection des droits de l'enfant?', *l.c.* (note 12), p. 5.

[183] *Cf.* reporting guidelines for Article 3(2) *juncto* Article 3(4) (note 181).

3.3 Article 3(3): Minimum Safeguards

51. Article 3(3)[184] contains the minimum safeguards that States Parties shall maintain when permitting voluntary recruitment of persons below the age of 18 years. In order to introduce an element of transparency, they must be set out in the binding declaration.[185] Without the fulfilment of the safeguards, no voluntary recruitment of under-18s is possible. Reports should provide information on their implementation,[186] which may be difficult in practice.[187] Moreover, few youngsters stating that they are volunteering will satisfy the criteria.[188]

First of all, the recruitment must be genuinely voluntary. No definition of 'genuinely' is provided.[189] In any case, it will not be easy to determine if this requirement is satisfied. Reports have to indicate a detailed description of the procedure used for the recruitment, i.e. from the expression of

---

[184] The reporting guidelines for Article 3(3) determine:
   'With regard to the minimum safeguards that States Parties shall maintain concerning voluntary recruitment, reports should provide information on the implementation of these safeguards and indicate among others:
   • A detailed description of the procedure used for such recruitment from the expression of intention to volunteer until the physical integration into the armed forces;
   • Medical examination foreseen before recruitment into the armed forces;
   • The reliable documentation to verify the age of the volunteers (birth certificates, affidavit, etc.);
   • Information that is made available to the volunteers, and to their parents or legal guardians allowing them to formulate their own opinion and to make them aware of the duties involved in the military service. A copy of any materials used for this information is to be annexed to the report;
   • The effective minimum service time and the conditions for early discharge; the use of military justice or discipline to under-18–years recruits and disaggregated data on the number of such recruits under-trial or in detention; the minimum and maximum sanctions foreseen in case of desertion;
   • The incentives used by the national armed forces for encouraging volunteers to join the ranks (scholarships, advertising, meetings at schools, games, etc.).'
[185] M. Happold, 'The Optional Protocol to the Convention on the Rights of the Child on the involvement of children in armed conflict', l.c. (note 32), p. 239.
[186] Reporting guidelines for Article 3(3) (note 185).
[187] Cf. D. Helle, 'Optional Protocol on the involvement of children in armed conflict to the Convention on the Rights of the Child', l.c. (note 26), p. 4; J. Mermet, 'Protocole facultatif à la Convention relative aux droits de l'enfant concernant l'implication d'enfants dans les conflits armés: quel progrès pour la protection des droits de l'enfant?', l.c. (note 12), p. 5. States should also avoid the early militarization of children: Cf. CRC Committee, Concluding Observations: Democratic People's Republic of Korea (UN Doc. CRC/C/Add. 239, 2004), para. 57; Myanmar (UN Doc. CRC/C/Add. 237, 2004), para. 66.
[188] R. Brett, 'Adolescents volunteering for armed forces or armed groups', International Review of the Red Cross 85, No 852, 2003, p. 864.
[189] Ibid.

intention to volunteer until the physical integration into the armed forces.[190] This could permit the CRC Committee to verify if a State effectively guarantees the control of the voluntary character and permits an eventual change of mind during the process.[191]

Secondly, the recruitment must be carried out with the informed consent of the person's parents or legal guardians. This obligation has been criticized. It is claimed that such consent is 'at best, irrelevant and, at worst, may be motivated by factors other than the parent's assessment of their child's best interests (for example, parents may encourage children to join the army to ease the strain on the family's budget)'.[192] This requirement demands that States inform the parents or legal guardians. It is not specified whether the consent should be done in written form or can be given orally.

Thirdly, the persons must be fully informed of the duties involved in such military service. Persons wishing to volunteer should thus be aware of their future duties in military service, which will allow them to formulate their opinion. The reporting guidelines demand that the same information is also provided to the parents or legal guardians.[193]

Fourthly, the persons must provide reliable proof of age prior to acceptance into national military service. This can for example be done through the presentation of birth certificates and affidavits.[194] Since many developing countries do not have good functioning birth registration systems, many people in war-affected countries will not be able to meet this condition.[195]

Reports should also contain certain information allowing the Committee to evaluate to which amount States influence youngsters to join and how easy it is to leave the armed forces when one changes his mind.

---

[190] Reporting guidelines for Article 3(3) (note 185).

[191] Interestingly, in its concluding observations, the Committee on the Rights of the Child recommended that the State Party 'take all necessary measures to ensure that Article 38(3) of the Convention is respected in order to ensure that recruitment is genuinely voluntary when recruiting children between 16 and 18, and that priority will be given to the oldest applicants' (CRC Committee, *Concluding Observations*: Democratic People's Republic of Korea (UN Doc. CRC/C/Add. 239, 2004), para. 57). The Committee thus seems to consider the priority rule as a means of ensuring the voluntary character of recruitment.

[192] A. Sheppard, 'Child soldiers: Is the optional protocol evidence of an emerging 'straight-18' consensus?', *l.c.* (note 22), p. 50.

[193] Reporting guidelines for Article 3(3) (note 185).

[194] *Ibid.*

[195] D. Helle, 'Optional Protocol on the involvement of children in armed conflict to the Convention on the Rights of the Child', *l.c.* (note 26), p. 4; J. Mermet, 'Protocole facultatif à la Convention relative aux droits de l'enfant concernant l'implication d'enfants dans les conflits armés: quel progrès pour la protection des droits de l'enfant?', *l.c.* (note 12), p. 5.

3.4   Article 3(4): Strengthening of Declaration

52. Pursuant to Article 3(4),[196] States may strengthen their declaration at any time by notification to that effect addressed to the Secretary-General of the United Nations. The Secretary-General shall then inform all States Parties to the Protocol. The notification takes effect on the date on which it is received by the Secretary-General. Hence, a State Party to the Optional Protocol can not reduce the minimum age from which it recruits, but it may increase this age.[197] When relevant, reports should indicate the national, regional, local, and other debates, initiatives or any campaign aiming at strengthening the declaration.[198]

3.5   Article 3(5): Military Schools

53. Article 3(5)[199] exempts military schools from the new rules on voluntary recruitment. It determines that the requirement to raise the minimum age in paragraph 1 does not apply to schools operated by or under the control of the armed forces of the States Parties, in keeping with Articles 28 and 29 of the CRC. This exception is very important since military schools are reserves of recruits in times of armed conflicts.[200] It finds it origins in the

---

[196] *Cf.* note 181.

[197] M. Happold, 'The Optional Protocol to the Convention on the Rights of the Child on the involvement of children in armed conflict', *l.c.* (note 32), p. 238.

[198] Reporting guidelines for Article 3(2) *juncto* Article 3(4) (note 181).

[199] The reporting guidelines for Article 3(5) determine:
'Reports should indicate, among others, information on:
- The minimum age of entry into schools operated by or under the control of the armed forces;
- Disaggregated data on schools operated by or under the control of the armed forces, including numbers, type of education, proportion between academic education and military training in the curricula; length of this education; academic/military personnel involved, educational facilities, *etc.*;
- The inclusion in the school curricula of human rights and humanitarian principles, including in areas relevant to the realisation of the rights of the child;
- Disaggregated data on the students in these schools (for example, by gender, age, region, rural/urban areas and social and ethnic origin); their status (members or not of the armed forces); their military status in the case of a mobilisation or of an armed conflict, a genuine military need or any other emergency situation; their right to leave such schools at any time and not to pursue a military career;
- All appropriate measures taken, to ensure that school discipline is administered in a manner consistent with the child's human dignity and any complaint mechanism available in this regard.'

[200] J. Mermet, 'Protocole facultatif à la Convention relative aux droits de l'enfant concernant l'implication d'enfants dans les conflits armés: quel progrès pour la protection des droits de l'enfant?', *l.c.* (note 12), p. 5.

argument of many countries that the function of military service is not limited to defence and that military schools give young people access to education.[201] From the start, there was substantial support for this kind of exemption.[202] It is uncertain which schools are targeted by the notion 'schools operated by or under the control of the armed forces of the States Parties'. Does it for example include schools operated by the ministry of defence but integral part of the general public education?[203]

54. States need to respect the Articles 28 and 29 of the CRC, although not all Parties to the Optional Protocol are Party to the CRC. Those Articles concern the right to education and the aims of education. Attention should for example be paid to the proportion between academic education and military training. The inclusion of human rights and humanitarian principles in the school curricula is also recommended. Another possible feature of this obligation is the administration of school discipline in a manner consistent with the child's human dignity.[204]

In its Concluding Observations relating to New Zealand, the Committee on the Right of the Child not only refers to Articles 28 and 29 of the CRC, but also to the aims of education as recognized in the Committee's general comment No 1.[205, 206]

55. The statute of the students in military schools (e.g. members or not of the armed forces, military status in case of emergency situations) is very important since the students become legitimate military targets if they are considered being members of the armed forces.[207] In their reports, States should provide information on this statute.

---

[201] Unicef, Guide, *o.c.* (note 54), p. 16. As J. Mermet rightly observes, it should be possible to use the money put at the disposition of these military schools for schools entirely operated by the civil administration (J. Mermet, 'Protocole facultatif à la Convention relative aux droits de l'enfant concernant l'implication d'enfants dans les conflits armés: quel progrès pour la protection des droits de l'enfant?', *l.c.* (note 12), p. 6); *Cf.* also D. Helle, 'Optional Protocol on the involvement of children in armed conflict to the Convention on the Rights of the Child', *l.c.* (note 26), p. 4.

[202] A. Sheppard, 'Child soldiers: Is the optional protocol evidence of an emerging 'straight-18'consensus?', *l.c.* (note 22), p. 51.

[203] *Cf.* J. Mermet, 'Protocole facultatif à la Convention relative aux droits de l'enfant concernant l'implication d'enfants dans les conflits armés: quel progrès pour la protection des droits de l'enfant?', *l.c.* (note 12), p. 6.

[204] Reporting guidelines for Article 3(5) (note 200).

[205] General Comment No 1, *The Aims of Education* (UN Doc. CRC/C/GC/2001/1, 2001).

[206] CRC Committee, *Concluding Observations: New Zealand* (UN Doc. CRC/C/OPAC/CO/2003/NZL, 2003), para. 8.

[207] J. Mermet, 'Protocole facultatif à la Convention relative aux droits de l'enfant concer-

It could be derived from the reporting guidelines that it is recommended that the students should also have the right to leave the military school at any time.[208]

4. Article 4: Armed Groups

56. In three paragraphs, Article 4 of the Optional Protocol[209] sets out a regime applicable to armed groups that are distinct from the armed groups of a State. The treatment of non-governmental actors was a major issue in the negotiations on the Protocol. A compromise text was adopted.[210] The importance of the provision lies in the fact that many child soldiers are recruited by rebel groups in internal conflicts, whereas the CRC only applies to States Parties.[211]

---

nant l'implication d'enfants dans les conflits armés: quel progrès pour la protection des droits de l'enfant?', *l.c.* (note 12), pp. 5–6.

[208] *Cf.* reporting guidelines for Article 3(5) (note 200).

[209] The reporting guidelines for Article 4 determine:
'Please provide information on, *inter alia*:
- The armed groups operating on/from the territory of the State concerned or with sanctuary on that territory;
- Update on the status of the negotiations of the State Party with the armed groups;
- Disaggregated data on children who have been recruited and used in hostilities by the armed groups, and on those who have been arrested by the State concerned (for example, by gender, age, region, rural/urban areas and social and ethnic origin, time spent in the armed groups, and time spent in hostilities);
- Any written or oral commitment made by armed groups aiming at not recruiting and using children below the age of 18 years in hostilities;
- Measures adopted by the State concerned aiming at raising awareness amongst armed groups and within the communities of the need to prevent recruitment of children below the age of 18 years and of their legal duties with regard to the minimum age set up in the Optional Protocol for recruitment and use in hostilities;
- The adoption of legal measures which aim at prohibiting and criminalizing the recruitment and use in hostilities of children under the age of 18 years by such armed groups and the judicial decisions applying to this issue;
- The programmes to prevent notably children who are at highest risk of recruitment or use by such armed groups, such as refugee and internally displaced children, street children, orphans (e.g. birth registration campaigns) from being recruited or used by armed groups.'

[210] *Cf.* for this discussion M. Dennis, 'The ILO Convention on the worst forms of child labor', *l.c.* (note 145), p. 792.

[211] International Committee of the Red Cross, 'Optional Protocol to the Convention on the Rights of the Child concerning the involvement of children in armed conflicts: Position of the International Committee of the Red Cross Geneva, 27 October 1997', *l.c.* (note 17), No 52; F. Grünfeld, 'Child soldiers', *l.c.* (note 133), p. 286.

4.1   Article 4(1): Recruitment or Use in Hostilities

57. Article 4(1) states that armed groups that are distinct from the armed groups of a State should not, under any circumstances, recruit or use in hostilities persons under the age of 18 years.

4.1.1   Armed groups that are distinct from the armed forces of a State
58. The notion 'armed groups that are distinct from the armed forces of a State' has not been defined.

References to 'armed groups' can be found in international humanitarian law. Article 1(1) of the second Additional Protocol to the Geneva Conventions lists various objective criteria which must be satisfied in order to qualify a group as an armed group.[212] The first criterion asks for responsible command. This implies a 'certain degree of organization sufficient to enable the group to conduct sustained and concerted military operations and to impose discipline'.[213] Secondly, the armed group should control a part of the territory. 'Control' is 'understood to mean domination of a part of the territory, but it is not specified what part of the territory should be controlled. The control must be sufficient to enable the armed group to conduct sustained and concerted military operations and to implement the Protocol'.[214] The third criterion of the sustained and concerted character of military operations is an 'objective criterion which takes no account of the duration or intensity of the operations. Such operations must not be sporadic and must be planned or prepared by organized armed groups capable of taking concerted action'.[215] A last criterion demands that the armed group has the ability to implement the Additional Protocol. If the definition is applicable in this context, that would be Article 4(1) of the Optional Protocol.

The armed groups must be 'distinct from the armed forces of a State'. According to M. HAPPOLD, 'the definition does not appear to be limited to insurgent armed groups in conflict with the governments of States Parties, but is wide enough to encompass armed groups allied with a State Party's government but not part of or under the control of its armed forces'.[216]

---

[212] Article 1(1); Cf. also International Committee of the Red Cross, 'Optional Protocol to the Convention on the Rights of the Child concerning the involvement of children in armed conflicts: Position of the International Committee of the Red Cross Geneva, 27 October 1997', l.c. (note 17), No 50.

[213] Ibid.

[214] Ibid.

[215] Ibid.

[216] M. Happold, 'The Optional Protocol to the Convention on the Rights of the Child on the involvement of children in armed conflict', l.c. (note 32), p. 239.

4.1.2 *Absolute moral obligation*

59. The mentioned armed groups should not, under any circumstances, recruit or use in hostilities persons under the age of 18 years. Any written or oral commitment made by armed groups in this regard should be indicated in the reports.[217] In 2002, the CRC Committee in its concluding observations relating to the CRC, has recommended that *all other relevant actors* than the State Party end all recruitment and use of children as soldiers.[218] This is an example of how the Committee's interpretation of the CRC is influenced by the content of the Optional Protocol.

60. The discussion on the different interpretations of 'recruitment' has been dealt with above (*Cf. supra* No 38). Article 4 does not distinguish between voluntary and compulsory recruitment, thus covering both. It also include cross-border recruitment,[219] which is often practised by rebel groups. Moreover, the Article targets all persons under the age of 18 years. Hence, contrary to States Parties, non-governmental armed groups are not allowed to voluntarily recruit persons between 16 and 18 years of age. The fact that governments are not bound by the same standard may undermine the Protocol,[220] since it is unlikely that armed groups are willing to obey rules that place them in a more constraining situation than their adversaries.[221] The prohibition is of a general nature. Armed groups are not required to be actively engaged in armed conflict before the article applies: it is also forbidden to recruit under-18s prior to the outbreak of hostilities.[222]

It is uncertain how 'use in hostilities' should be interpreted. The notion seems to be broader than 'direct participation in hostilities'[223] (*Cf. supra* No

---

[217] Reporting guidelines for Article 4 (note 210).

[218] CRC Committee, *Concluding Observations*: Sudan (UN Doc. CRC/C/Add. 190, 2002), para. 60, emphasis added.

[219] This could *inter alia* be derived from the Preamble ('within and across national borders') and from the recommendations of the Committee on the Rights of the Child in CRC Committee, *Concluding Observations*: Democratic Republic of the Congo (UN Doc. CRC/C/Add. 153, 2001), para. 65.

[220] G. Machel, *The impact of armed conflict on children*, (UN Doc. A/51/306, 1996); *Cf.* Unicef, Guide, *o.c.* (note 54), p. 17.

[221] J. Mermet, 'Protocole facultatif à la Convention relative aux droits de l'enfant concernant l'implication d'enfants dans les conflits armés: quel progrès pour la protection des droits de l'enfant?', *l.c.* (note 12), p. 6; D. Helle, 'Optional Protocol on the involvement of children in armed conflict to the Convention on the Rights of the Child', *l.c.* (note 26), p. 5.

[222] Unicef, Guide, *o.c.* (note 54), p. 17.

[223] *Cf.* Article 38 of the Convention on the Rights of the Child, Article 1 of the Optional Protocol to the Convention on the Rights of the Child on the involvement of children in armed conflict, Article 77(2) of the first Additional Protocol to the Geneva Conventions and Article 3 of the second Additional Protocol to the Geneva Conventions.

28–32) and than 'use to participate actively in hostilities'[224] (*Cf. supra* No 12). Indeed, as was already mentioned, the notion 'use to participate actively' is wider than direct participation, but is more specific than 'use in hostilities'. The CRC Committee will hopefully provide a clear definition of the term.

61. In contrast to the more complex provisions regarding State recruitment into the (national) armed forces, the prohibition for armed groups is absolute:[225] they should not, *under any circumstances*, recruit under-18s or use them in hostilities. However, the Protocol uses the term 'should not' instead of 'must not' or 'shall not',[226] thereby weakening the scope of the obligation.[227] This reflects the traditional view that only States have obligations under international human rights law, whereas the behaviour of non-state entities is to be regulated by domestic law.[228] Hence, rebel groups are under a moral rather than a legal obligation.[229,230] Ensuring compliance by non-state parties will thus be difficult,[231] most certainly given the fact that such armed groups are almost always illegal as such.[232]

---

[224] *Cf.* Article 8 of the Rome Statute of the International Criminal Court.

[225] M. Happold, 'The Optional Protocol to the Convention on the Rights of the Child on the involvement of children in armed conflict', *l.c.* (note 32), p. 239.

[226] Unicef, Guide, *o.c.* (note 54), p. 17.

[227] J. Mermet, 'Protocole facultatif à la Convention relative aux droits de l'enfant concernant l'implication d'enfants dans les conflits armés: quel progrès pour la protection des droits de l'enfant?', *l.c.*(note 12), p. 4.

[228] Unicef, Guide, *o.c.* (note 54), p. 17; J. Mermet, 'Protocole facultatif à la Convention relative aux droits de l'enfant concernant l'implication d'enfants dans les conflits armés: quel progrès pour la protection des droits de l'enfant?', *l.c.* (note 12), p. 4; D. Helle, 'Optional Protocol on the involvement of children in armed conflict to the Convention on the Rights of the Child', *l.c.* (note 26), p. 4.

[229] J. Mermet, 'Protocole facultatif à la Convention relative aux droits de l'enfant concernant l'implication d'enfants dans les conflits armés: quel progrès pour la protection des droits de l'enfant?', *l.c.* (note 12), p. 4; D. Helle, 'Optional Protocol on the involvement of children in armed conflict to the Convention on the Rights of the Child', *l.c.* (note 26), p. 4.

[230] Mexico issued the following interpretative declaration in this regard:
'Any responsibility deriving for non-governmental armed groups for the recruitment of children under 18 years or their use in hostilities lies solely with such groups and shall not be applicable to the Mexican State as such. The latter shall have a duty to apply at all times the principles governing international humanitarian law.'

[231] A. Sheppard, 'Child soldiers: Is the optional protocol evidence of an emerging 'straight-18'consensus?', *l.c.* (note 22), p. 53.

[232] J. Mermet, 'Protocole facultatif à la Convention relative aux droits de l'enfant concernant l'implication d'enfants dans les conflits armés: quel progrès pour la protection des droits de l'enfant?', *l.c.* (note 12), p. 4.

4.2   Article 4(2): Prevention

62. Article 4(2) concerns the prevention of the recruitment and use of under-18s by non-governmental armed groups. States Parties shall take all feasible measures to prevent this.

4.2.1   Prevention of such recruitment and use

63. States Parties shall prevent 'such recruitment and use'. The provision clearly refers to Article 4(1), thereby implying that States Parties shall prevent the recruitment and use of persons under the age of 18 years by armed groups that are distinct from the armed forces of a State. In its reporting guidelines, the Committee on the Rights of the Child asks States to provide information on the armed groups operating on or from the territory of the State concerned or with sanctuary on that territory.[233] The obligation thus seems to comprehend all those groups.

4.2.2   Obligation of means resting on States Parties

64. All feasible measures shall be taken by States Parties. Hence, in accordance with traditional international law,[234] Article 4(2) imposes a duty on all States Parties to regulate the behaviour of armed groups.[235]

As discussed above, the use of the term 'all feasible measures' implies that States are under an obligations of means (*Cf. supra* No 34–36). The phrase thus recognizes that States frequently lack control or influence over armed groups operating in their territory.[236] Moreover, other States may support or influence such groups and armed groups sometimes recruit from the territory of States that are not party to the conflict.[237] Prevention is easier when armed groups allied with the government but not part of or under the control of its armed forces are concerned.[238] Interestingly, in its recent Concluding Observations relating to a report of Rwanda under the CRC, the CRC Committee recommended that 'the State take all *necessary* measures to ensure that no under-18s are recruited into the Local Defence Forces

---

[233] Reporting guidelines for Article 4 (note 210).
[234] F. Grünfeld, 'Child soldiers', *l.c.* (note 133), p. 285.
[235] Unicef, Guide, *o.c.* (note 54), p. 17.
[236] M. Happold, 'The Optional Protocol to the Convention on the Rights of the Child on the involvement of children in armed conflict', *l.c.* (note 32), p. 239.
[237] M. Dennis, 'The ILO Convention on the worst forms of child labor', *l.c.* (note 145), p. 793.
[238] M. Happold, 'The Optional Protocol to the Convention on the Rights of the Child on the involvement of children in armed conflict', *l.c.* (note 32), p. 239.

or in any armed group proceeding to recruitment on the territory of the State Party'.[239]

65. Article 4(2) contains at least one indication about the concrete measures that States could take: they need to adopt legal measures necessary to prohibit and criminalize such practices. In its concluding observations relating to reports submitted under the CRC, the CRC Committee also recommended that States Parties should establish and strictly enforce legislation prohibiting the future recruitment[240] and criminalizing the recruitment and use[241] of children by any armed forces or armed group. With regard to Indonesia, it asked the State 'to ensure that all persons, including senior officials, who have sponsored, planned, incited, financed or participated in military or paramilitary operations using child soldiers will be appropriately prosecuted'.[242]

Criminal repression will however not be sufficient to meet the obligation of prevention.[243] States therefore need to take additional measures. It could be derived from the reporting guidelines that States should set up prevention programmes for children who are at highest risk of recruitment and use (such as refugee and internally displaced children, street children and orphans).[244] In this regard, the concluding observations of the CRC Committee, recommending States to provide alternatives for military recruitment, such as increasing employment and education opportunities for adolescents and young people in both urban and rural areas,[245] specifically for vulnerable children in refugee diaspora and tribal areas,[246] are particularly relevant. Awareness raising campaigns are also an important aspect of prevention. As such, the CRC Committee in its concluding observations relating to the

---

[239] CRC Committee, *Concluding Observations:* Rwanda (UN Doc. CRC/C/Add. 234, 2004), para. 63, emphasis added.

[240] CRC Committee, *Concluding Observations:* Sierra Leone (UN Doc. CRC/C/Add. 116, 2000), para. 73; Colombia (UN Doc. CRC/C/Add. 137, 2000), para. 56; *Cf.* also CRC Committee, *Concluding Observations:* Paraguay (UN Doc. CRC/C/Add. 166, 2001), para. 46(a), in which the Committee urges the State Party to punish those involved in forcible recruitment.

[241] CRC Committee, *Concluding Observations:* Indonesia (UN Doc. CRC/C/Add. 223, 2004), para. 72.

[242] *Ibid.*, para. 71.

[243] D. Helle, 'Optional Protocol on the involvement of children in armed conflict to the Convention on the Rights of the Child', *l.c.* (note 26), p. 4.

[244] Reporting guidelines for Article 4 (note 210).

[245] CRC Committee, *Concluding Observations:* Mozambique (UN Doc. CRC/C/Add. 172, 2002), para. 63.

[246] CRC Committee, *Concluding Observations:* Indonesia (UN Doc. CRC/C/Add. 223, 2004), para. 72.

CRC already recommended that awareness raising campaigns for army officials be undertaken.[247]

In case prevention was not sufficient, States should, according to the CRC Committee, ask in the context of peace negotiations that opposition armed forces cease to use children as soldiers.[248] Reports should provide an update on the negotiations with the armed groups.[249]

4.3   Article 4(3): Legal Status of the Parties

66. Article 4(3) reflects the compromise reached in adopting the provisions on armed groups. It states that the application of the article shall not affect the legal status of any party to an armed conflict. As the ICRC repeatedly stressed, it is a fundamental principle of international humanitarian law that all parties to a conflict must be treated on foot of equality.[250] This equality must be respected even in the absence of reciprocity in the application of international humanitarian law. One of the direct consequences of the principle is the fact that the application of international humanitarian law has no effect on the legal status of parties to a conflict,[251] and thus 'in no way changes the legal status—whether or not contested by the adverse party—that a party had when the conflict broke out, and neither establishes nor consolidates an attribute which did not previously exist'.[252] As far as Article 4 of the Optional Protocol is concerned, this also applies to human rights law.

5. Article 5: Safeguard Clause

67. Article 5 of the Optional Protocol[253] contains a safeguard clause. Nothing in the Protocol shall be construed as precluding provisions of the law of a

---

[247] CRC Committee, *Concluding Observations: Cambodia* (UN Doc. CRC/C/Add. 128, 2000), para. 59.

[248] CRC Committee, *Concluding Observations: Burundi* (CRC/C/Add. 133, 2000), para. 72.

[249] Reporting guidelines for Article 4 (note 210).

[250] A. Sheppard, 'Child soldiers: Is the optional protocol evidence of an emerging 'straight-18'consensus?', *l.c.* (note 22), p. 53.

[251] International Committee of the Red Cross, 'Optional Protocol to the Convention on the Rights of the Child concerning the involvement of children in armed conflicts: Position of the International Committee of the Red Cross Geneva, 27 October 1997', *l.c.* (note 17), No 46.

[252] *Ibid.*, No 51.

[253] The reporting guidelines for Article 5 determine:
'Please indicate any provision of national legislation and of international instruments and international humanitarian law applicable in the state concerned, which are more conducive to the realisation of the rights of the child. Reports should also pro-

State Party or in international instruments and international humanitarian law that are more conducive to the realization of the rights of the child. They should also provide information on the main international instruments concerning children in armed conflict and on other commitments undertaken by the State concerning this issue.[254] The Optional Protocol thus allows States to bind themselves to standards that surpass those outlined in the Protocol whether through national legislation and other international treaties.[255] This is also a general principle of international law.[256] Reports should indicate these provisions.[257] For example, States having chosen to adopt a 'straight 18'-policy concerning recruitment, or States Parties to the African Charter on the Rights and Welfare of the Child will be bound by these higher standards.[258] A similar safeguard clause can be found in Article 41 of the CRC.

6. Article 6: Implementation, Dissemination, Demobilisation and Recovery

68. Article 6 is a key Article of the Optional Protocol. The first paragraph deals with implementation and enforcement whereas the second paragraph tackles the dissemination of the Protocol. The third, very important, paragraph of Article 6 emphasizes the need for demobilisation and recovery of child soldiers.

6.1   Article 6(1): Implementation and Enforcement

69. Article 6(1)[259] determines that States Parties shall take all necessary measures to ensure the implementation and enforcement of the Protocol within

---

vide information on the status of ratification by the State concerned of the main international instruments concerning children in armed conflict and on other commitments undertaken by that State concerning this issue.'

[254] *Ibid.*

[255] Unicef, Guide, *o.c.* (note 54), p. 18.

[256] *Cf. ibid.*

[257] Reporting guidelines for Article 5 (note 254).

[258] *Ibid.*

[259] The reporting guidelines for Article 6(1) *juncto* Article 6(2) determine:
'Please indicate the measures adopted to ensure the effective implementation and enforcement of the provisions of the Optional Protocol within the jurisdiction of the State Party, including information on:
  • Any review of domestic legislation and amendments introduced to it;
  • The legal status of the Optional Protocol in national law and its applicability before domestic jurisdictions, as well as, when relevant, the intention of the State Party to withdraw existing reservations made to this Protocol;
  • The competent governmental departments or bodies responsible for the implemen-

their jurisdiction. The provision is to be read together with Article 6(2) concerning the dissemination of the Protocol.[260] Indeed, dissemination is an essential means of educating people on the Optional Protocol and will thus contribute to its application.

70. All necessary measures need to be taken. Since the term 'necessary' only refers to the aim contemplated, whereas 'feasible' also refers to the circumstances,[261] States are under an absolute obligation. Measures can be of a legal, administrative or other nature. No further indication is given about the kind of measures to be adopted. The result however needs to be the *effective* implementation and enforcement. A review of domestic legislation or amendments introduced to it, may prove necessary.[262]

It is recommended that competent governmental departments or bodies responsible for the implementation of the Optional Protocol co-operate with regional and local authorities as well as with civil society. Moreover, mechanisms could be put in place for monitoring and periodically evaluating the implementation of the Protocol.[263]

71. Pursuant to Article 4 of the CRC, States shall undertake all appropriate legislative, administrative, and other measures for the implementation of the rights recognized in the Convention. With regard to economic, social and cultural rights, States Parties shall undertake such measures to the maximum extent of their available resources and, where needed, within the framework of international co-operation. Article 6(1) of the Optional Protocol is clearly more stringent. The use of the terms 'to undertake' and 'appropriate measures' and the budgetary restraint for the implementation of economic, social and cultural rights in the CRC are but some of the arguments to come to this conclusion.

---

tation of the Optional Protocol and their coordination with regional and local authorities as well as with civil society;
  • The mechanisms and means used for monitoring and periodically evaluating the implementation of the Optional Protocol;
  • Measures adopted to ensure the relevant training of peacekeeping personnel on the rights of the child, including the provisions of the Optional Protocol;
  • The dissemination in all relevant languages of the Optional Protocol to all children and adults, notably those responsible for military recruitment, and the appropriate training offered to all professional groups working with and for children.'
  [260] *Cf.* reporting guidelines for Article 6(1) *juncto* Article 6(2) (note 260).
  [261] M. Happold, 'The Optional Protocol to the Convention on the Rights of the Child on the involvement of children in armed conflict', *l.c.* (note 130), p. 34.
  [262] *Cf.* reporting guidelines for Article 6(1) *juncto* Article 6(2) (note 261); Unicef, Guide, *o.c.* (note 54), p. 41.
  [263] Reporting guidelines for Article 6(1) *juncto* Article 6(2) (note 261).

6.2   Article 6(2): Dissemination

72. According to Article 6(2),[264] States Parties undertake to make the principles and provisions of the Protocol widely known and promoted[265] by appropriate means, to adults and children alike. This obligation of dissemination can notably be seen as one of the means to implement the Protocol (*Cf. supra* No 69).[266]

In its usual meaning, 'to undertake' implies that someone promises to do something, begins to do it, or does it.[267] Hence, it is not required that that something is also accomplished. This obligation is thus weaker than an obligation using the term 'shall'.

Anyone should be informed of the Protocol, adults and children, all layers of society. This needs to be done by all appropriate means. Towards children, school curricula can be a useful way of dissemination.[268] For peacekeeping personnel,[269] other military personnel[270] and all other professional groups working with and for children,[271] relevant training is to be ensured. Moreover, it is recommended to publish and widely distribute the initial reports and concluding observations.[272] This can generate debate and awareness as well as implementation and monitoring.[273]

73. The Convention on the Rights of the Child in its Article 42 determines that States Parties undertake to make the principles and provisions of the Convention widely known, by appropriate and active means, to adults and children alike. This provision is very similar to Article 6(2) but it does not state that the principles and provisions should be promoted. Moreover, appropriate and *active* means are to be used. The CRC thus emphasizes the active attitude to be adopted by States and their eventual positive obligations.

---

[264] *Cf.* note 260.

[265] In the French version no mention is made of 'promote': 'Les Etats Parties s'engagent à faire largement *connaître* les principes et dispositions du Protocole' (emphasis added). The term thus does not seem to add something to the obligation contained in Article 6(2).

[266] *Cf.* reporting guidelines: they mention Article 6(2) together with Article 6(1).

[267] *Cf.* several dictionary definitions.

[268] CRC Committee, *Concluding Observations:* New Zealand (UN Doc. CRC/C/OPAC/CO/2003/NZL, 2003), para. 10.

[269] *Cf.* reporting guidelines for Article 6(1) *juncto* Article 6(2) (note 260).

[270] CRC Committee, *Concluding Observations:* New Zealand (UN Doc. CRC/C/OPAC/CO/2003/NZL, 2003), para. 10.

[271] Reporting guidelines for Article 6(1) *juncto* Article 6(2) (note 260).

[272] CRC Committee, *Concluding Observations:* New Zealand (UN Doc. CRC/C/OPAC/CO/2003/NZL, 2003), para. 11.

[273] *Ibid.*

6.3   Article 6(3): Demobilisation and Recovery

The important Article 6(3)[274] concerns the demobilisation and recovery of child soldiers, thus giving effect to a number of recommendations out of, *inter alia*, the Machel report.[275] States Parties shall take all feasible measures to ensure that persons within their jurisdiction recruited or used in hostilities contrary to the Protocol are demobilized or otherwise released from service. Moreover, when necessary, they shall accord to such persons all appropriate assistance for their physical and psychological recovery and their social reintegration. The need to rehabilitate and reintegrate children had only recently been recognized in international law,[276] in particular in Article 39 of the CRC (*Cf. supra* No 11).[277] However, it was not until the

---

[274] The reporting guidelines for Article 6(3) determine:
'When relevant, please indicate all measures adopted with regard to disarmament, demobilisation (or release from service) and the provision of appropriate assistance for the physical and psychological recovery and social reintegration of children, taking due account of the situation of girls, including information on:
• Disaggregated data on children involved in that proceeding, on their participation in such programmes, and on their status with regard to the armed forces and armed groups (e.g. when do they stop to be members of the armed forces or groups?);
• The budget allocated to these programmes, the personnel involved and their training, the organization concerned, cooperation among them, and participation of civil society, local communities, families, *etc.*;
• The various measures adopted to ensure the social reintegration of children, e.g. interim care, access to education and vocational training, reintegration in the family and community, relevant judicial measures, while taking into account the specific needs of children concerned depending notably on their age and sex;
• The measures adopted to ensure confidentiality and protection of children involved in such programmes from media exposure and exploitation;
• The legal provisions adopted criminalizing the recruitment of children and the inclusion of that crime in the competence of any specific justice seeking mechanisms established in the context of conflict (e.g. war crimes tribunal, truth and reconciliation bodies). The safeguards adopted to ensure that the rights of the child as a victim and as a witness are respected in these mechanisms in light of the Convention on the Rights of the Child;
• The criminal liability of children for crimes they may have committed during their stay with armed forces or groups and the judicial procedure applicable, as well as safeguards to ensure that the rights of the child are respected;
a When relevant, the provisions of peace agreements dealing with disarmament, demobilization and/or physical and psychological recovery and social reintegration of child combatants.'
[275] G. Machel, *o.c.* (note 221); M. Happold, 'The Optional Protocol to the Convention on the Rights of the Child on the involvement of children in armed conflict', *l.c.* (note 32), p. 240.
[276] R. Harvey, *o.c.* (note 7), p. 32.
[277] *Cf. inter alia*, CRC Committee, *Concluding Observations:* Yemen (UN Doc. CRC/C/Add. 102, 1999), para. 31; Nicaragua (UN Doc. CRC/C/Add. 108, 1999), para. 38; Russian Federation (UN Doc. CRC/C/Add. 110, 1999), para. 57; Sierra Leone (UN Doc. CRC/C/Add. 116, 2000), para. 73; Armenia (UN Doc. CRC/C/Add. 119, 2000), para. 49; Georgia (UN Doc. CRC/C/Add. 124,

Optional Protocol that a binding international agreement explicitly imposed the obligation to demobilise, rehabilitate and reintegrate children who have been recruited or used in hostilities. In order to address the lack of resources to do this, the Optional Protocol obligates States to cooperate through technical and financial assistance (*Cf. infra* No 84–86).[278] Through international programmes, long-term assistance should be planned.[279] The CRC Committee also recommended international mediation.[280] Recently, the Committee urged Liberia,[281] Myanmar[282] and Rwanda[283] to take every feasible measure to have all present and former child soldiers released and demobilized and to rehabilitate them into their communities and in society taking into account particularly the specific needs of girls and other vulnerable groups.

Unfortunately, armed forces and armed groups rarely acknowledge the presence of children in their ranks,[284] what causes them to be excluded from the benefits attached to programmes for disarmament, demobilisation and reintegration (DDR programmes)[285, 286] Indeed, since the elements of those

---

2000), para. 59; Tajikistan (UN Doc. CRC/C/Add. 136, 2000), para. 47; Guatemala (UN Doc. CRC/C/Add. 154, 2001), para. 49; Bhutan (UN Doc. CRC/C/Add. 157, 2001), para. 57(b); Uzbekistan (UN Doc. CRC/C/Add. 167, 2001), para. 62(b).

[278] R. Harvey, *o.c.* (note 7), p. 32.

[279] Security Council Resolution S/2000/101, 11 February 2000, The Role of United Nations Peacekeeping in Disarmament, Demobilisation and Reintegration, No 92.

[280] *Cf.* CRC Committee, *Concluding Observations:* Cambodia (UN Doc. CRC/C/Add. 128, 2000), para. 59; Comores (UN Doc. CRC/C/Add. 141, 2000), para. 46; Democratic Republic of the Congo (UN Doc. CRC/C/Add. 153, 2001), para. 65; Sudan (UN Doc. CRC/C/Add. 190, 2002), para. 60.

[281] CRC Committee, *Concluding Observations:* Liberia (UN Doc. CRC/C/Add. 236, 2004), para. 59(a).

[282] CRC Committee, *Concluding Observations:* Myanmar (UN Doc. CRC/C/Add. 237, 2004), para. 67(b).

[283] CRC Committee, *Concluding Observations:* Rwanda (UN Doc. CRC/C/Add. 234, 2004), para. 63(b).

[284] United Nations Department of Peacekeeping Operations, *Disarmament, Demobilisation and Reintegration of Ex-combatants in a Peacekeeping Environment. Principles and Guidelines* (New York, United Nations Department of Peacekeeping Operations/Lessons Learned Unit, New York, 1999), No 31. An estimated 30 percent of the child combatants routinely do not enter the formal DDR process (No 195); Security Council Resolution S/2000/101, 11 February 2000, The Role of United Nations Peacekeeping in Disarmament, Demobilisation and Reintegration, No 23.

[285] DDR programmes are programmes for Disarmament, Demobilisation and Reintegration— also called DDRR programmes being Disarmament, Demobilisation, Reintegration and Rehabilitation.

[286] *Cf.* United Nations Department of Peacekeeping Operations, *o.c.* (note 285), No 31; Security Council Resolution S/2000/101, 11 February 2000, The Role of United Nations Peacekeeping in Disarmament, Demobilisation and Reintegration, No 23.

programmes overlap and are intrinsically linked,[287] this continuum can only begin at the moment of recognition of the problem.

6.3.1   Demobilize or otherwise release from service

75. According to the first obligation in Article 6(3), States shall take all feasible measures to ensure that persons within their jurisdiction recruited or used in hostilities contrary to the Protocol are demobilized or otherwise released from service.

76. The notion 'demobilize or otherwise release from service' has not been defined.

Roughly stated, demobilisation is 'the process of converting a soldier to a civilian'.[288] It is 'the process by which armed forces (government and/or opposition or factional forces) either downsize or completely disband, as part of a broader transformation from war to peace'.[289] Demobilisation thus seems to demand a formal procedure. There are also other ways to release children from service. As appears from the French version, using 'démobiliser ou de quelque autre manière libérer des obligations militaires', the aim pursued by Article 6(3) is that the children concerned are liberated from military obligations, regardless of the way to achieve this.

Many DDR processes require children to surrender their weapons to be eligible for the programmes. This has caused the exclusion of some children, especially of girls, who weren't in the possession of a weapon. Hence, it is recommended that DDR programmes do not demand children to hand in weapons as a condition for entering the program.[290] Moreover, special measures must be adopted to ensure that girls are not left out, especially those who have been abducted or sexually exploited.[291] This has also been emphasized by the Security Council in its resolutions concerning children and armed conflicts (Cf. supra No 16).

---

[287] Security Council Resolution S/2000/101, 11 February 2000, The Role of United Nations Peacekeeping in Disarmament, Demobilisation and Reintegration, No 8.

[288] K.M. Clark, 'The demobilisation and reintegration of soldiers: Perspectives from USAID', Africa Today 42, 1995, pp. 1–2.

[289] United Nations Department of Peacekeeping Operations, o.c. (note 285), No 14; Cf. also Security Council Resolution S/2000/101, 11 February 2000, The Role of United Nations Peacekeeping in Disarmament, Demobilisation and Reintegration, No 6(b): 'Demobilisation refers to the process by which parties to a conflict begin to disband their military structures and combatants begin the transformation into civilian life'.

[290] Security Council Resolution S/2000/101, 11 February 2000, The Role of United Nations Peacekeeping in Disarmament, Demobilisation and Reintegration, No 53.

[291] Unicef, Guide, o.c. (note 54), p. 41; Cf. also reporting guidelines for Article 4 (note 200).

It is important that demobilized children are dispersed or transferred as soon as possible to an interim care site or centre under civilian control,[292] and be separated from adult soldiers.[293] Once they are in civilian care, child protection agencies and other international institutions[294] need to be involved in providing them with health care, counselling and psycho-social support (*Cf. infra* No 79–83).[295]

77. Article 6(3) targets all persons within a State Party's jurisdiction recruited or used in hostilities contrary to the Protocol. For the armed forces, the targeted persons are under-18s directly participating in hostilities or compulsorily recruited, persons younger than 16 years voluntarily recruited and persons between 16 and 18 years voluntarily recruited in violation of the minimum safeguards. As far as non-governmental armed groups are concerned, all under-18s recruited or used in hostilities are targeted. Those persons must be under a State Party's jurisdiction. States are thus also responsible for children who have been recruited by any party, including on the territory of another State, but who are now within their jurisdiction,[296] as there are—as could be derived from the Concluding Observations relating to New Zealand—refugee and migrant children who have been involved in hostilities in their home countries.[297]

78. 'All feasible measures' are to be taken. As has been discussed above, this is an obligation of means (*Cf. infra* No 34–35). The measures need to be effective.[298] When concluding peace agreements for example, States should include provisions dealing with DDR programmes for child combatants.[299] Those provisions should also target opposition armed forces.[300] The role of chil-

---

[292] United Nations Department of Peacekeeping Operations, *o.c.* (note 285), No 184.

[293] *Ibid.*, No 193.

[294] Unicef, Guide, *o.c.* (note 54), p. 42.

[295] United Nations Department of Peacekeeping Operations, *o.c.* (note 285), No 184; Unicef, Guide, *o.c.* (note 54), p. 41.

[296] Unicef, Guide, *o.c.* (note 54), p. 41. This is also a general principle of international law and is stated in Article 2 of the CRC.

[297] In its Concluding Observations relating to New Zealand, the Committee on the Rights of the Child requests the State to provide information in its next report on refugee and migrant children within its jurisdiction who may have been involved in hostilities in their home country: *Cf.* CRC Committee, *Concluding Observations*: New Zealand (UN Doc. CRC/C/OPAC/CO/2003/NZL, 2003), para. 9.

[298] CRC Committee, *Concluding Observations*: Cambodia (UN Doc. CRC/C/Add. 128, 2000), para. 59; Colombia (UN Doc. CRC/C/Add. 137, 2000), para. 56.

[299] Reporting guidelines for Article 6(3) (note 276).

[300] CRC Committee, *Concluding Observations*: Burundi (UN Doc. CRC/C/Add. 133, 2000), para. 72.

dren in armed conflict is indeed to be acknowledged from the onset of peace negotiations,[301] and the demobilisation and reintegration of child combatants prioritised.[302] It can also be possible to demobilize child soldiers during conflicts.[303]

6.3.2 Recovery and reintegration

79. The second part of Article 6(3) determines that States Parties shall, when necessary, accord to such persons all appropriate assistance for their physical and psychological recovery and their social reintegration. The CRC Committee in its concluding observations regarding the CRC also emphasizes the need to assess and respond to the needs of child soldiers in terms of psychological assistance and to ensure family and social reintegration,[304] if necessary through international co-operation.[305]

80. Appropriate assistance should be accorded to 'such persons'. This term refers to the first sentence of Article 6(3), thus meaning persons within a State Party's jurisdiction recruited or used in hostilities contrary to the Protocol and demobilized or otherwise released from service.

81. The Optional Protocol does not specify what is to be understood by recovery and reintegration. Generally spoken, reintegration is 'the process of facilitating the ex-soldiers' transition to civilian life'.[306] Reintegration programmes are 'assistance measures provided to former combatants that would increase the potential for their and their families' economic and social reintegration into civil society. They could include cash assistance or compensation in kind, as well as vocation training and income-generating activities'.[307]

---

[301] Security Council Resolution S/2000/101, 11 February 2000, The Role of United Nations Peacekeeping in Disarmament, Demobilisation and Reintegration, No 18; *Cf.* also CRC Committee, *Concluding Observations:* Ethiopia (UN Doc. CRC/C/Add. 144, 2001), para. 69; Democratic Republic of the Congo (UN Doc. CRC/C/Add. 153, 2001), para. 65; Sudan (UN Doc. CRC/C/Add. 190, 2002), para. 60(c); Myanmar (UN Doc. CRC/C/Add. 237, 2004), para. 67(a).

[302] Security Council Resolution S/2000/101, 11 February 2000, The Role of United Nations Peacekeeping in Disarmament, Demobilisation and Reintegration; *Cf.* also CRC Committee, *Concluding Observations:* Myanmar (UN Doc. CRC/C/Add. 237, 2004), para. 67(b).

[303] United Nations Department of Peacekeeping Operations, *o.c.* (note 285), No 180.

[304] CRC Committee, *Concluding Observations:* Guinea-Bissau (UN Doc. CRC/C/Add. 177, 2002), para. 49; *Cf.* also CRC Committee, *Concluding Observations:* Niger (UN Doc. CRC/C/Add. 179, 2002), para. 63.

[305] CRC Committee, *Concluding Observations:* Azerbaijan (UN Doc. CRC/C/Add. 77, 1997), para. 48. *Cf.* also CRC Committee, *Concluding Observations:* Chad (UN Doc. CRC/C/Add. 107, 1999), para. 35; Burundi (UN Doc. CRC/C/Add. 133, 2000), para. 72.

[306] K.M. Clark, 'The demobilisation and reintegration of soldiers: Perspectives from USAID', *l.c.* (note 289), p. 2.

[307] United Nations Department of Peacekeeping Operations, *o.c.* (note 285), No 16; *Cf.* also

Since most child soldiers are physically (e.g. child amputees)[308] and psychologically marked, their recovery should be included in DDR programmes. Indeed, psycho-social support should not be reduced to individual psychological assistance but forms part of social reintegration.[309] Other social reintegration measures notably include interim care, access to education and vocational training, reintegration in the family and community and relevant judicial measures.[310] When adopting measures, due account should be taken, as was already mentioned, of the situation of girls and other vulnerable groups. It could also be encouraged to let civil society, local communities and families participate.[311] Compensation and support services to traumatized or permanently disabled child soldiers should also be provided.[312]

A first priority is family tracing, reunification[313] and reconciliation: through traditional forgiveness rituals and ceremonies, child soldiers can be accepted back into their families and communities.[314] Other actions that need to be taken include, as was already mentioned, educational opportunities,[315] 'catch-up' learning,[316] life skill and vocational training,[317] health care,[318] psychological support[319] and community development projects.[320] These are indeed the most effective ways to reintegrate children and to help provide a sta-

---

Security Council Resolution S/2000/101, 11 February 2000, The Role of United Nations Peacekeeping in Disarmament, Demobilisation and Reintegration, No 6(c): 'Reintegration refers to the process which allows ex-combatants and their families to adapt, economically and socially, to productive civilian life. It generally entails the provision of a package of cash or in-kind compensation, training and job-and income-generating projects.'

[308] *Cf.* CRC Committee, *Concluding Observations:* Sierra Leone (UN Doc. CRC/C/Add. 116, 2000), para. 74; Colombia (UN Doc. CRC/C/Add. 137, 2000), para. 57; Comores (UN Doc. CRC/C/Add. 141, 2000), para. 46.

[309] *Cf.* United Nations Department of Peacekeeping Operations, *o.c.* (note 285), No 189.

[310] *Ibid.*

[311] Reporting guidelines for Article 6(3) (note 276).

[312] CRC Committee, *Concluding Observations:* Chad (UN Doc. CRC/C/Add. 107, 1999), para. 35.

[313] Unicef, Guide, *o.c.* (note 54), p. 41; *Cf.* also United Nations Department of Peacekeeping Operations, *o.c.* (note 285), No 197 and No 200.

[314] Unicef, Guide, *o.c.* (note 54), p. 42.

[315] CRC Committee, *Concluding Observations:* Solomon Islands (UN Doc. CRC/C/Add. 208, 2003), para. 51; Indonesia (UN Doc. CRC/C/Add. 223, 2004), para. 72; Myanmar (UN Doc. CRC/C/Add. 237, 2004), para. 67(f).

[316] Unicef, Guide, *o.c.* (note 54), p. 42.

[317] *Ibid.*

[318] CRC Committee, *Concluding Observations:* Solomon Islands (UN Doc. CRC/C/Add. 208, 2003), para. 51; Indonesia (UN Doc. CRC/C/Add. 223, 2004), para. 72; Myanmar (UN Doc. CRC/C/Add. 237, 2004), para. 67(f).

[319] Unicef, Guide, *o.c.* (note 54), p. 42.

[320] *Ibid.*

ble environment within the community.[321] Relating to education, States also need to provide non-formal education programmes by prioritising the rehabilitation of school buildings and facilities and the provision of water, sanitation and electricity in conflict-affected areas.[322]

Justice is also considered a means of recovery and reintegration by the CRC Committee. Legal provisions should be adopted to criminalize the recruitment of children and that crime could eventually be included in the competence of notably war crimes tribunals and truth and reconciliation bodies.[323] The rights of the child as a victim and as a witness are then to be respected.[324] One could for example think of the participation rights of children contained in Article 12 of the CRC. In some instances, children could also be criminally liable for crimes they may have committed during their stay with armed forces or groups.[325] Children should also be provided just and adequate reparation.[326]

82. The measures taken need to be effective.[327] They should preferably be situated within the framework of long-term and comprehensive programmes of assistance, rehabilitation and reintegration for all children affected by armed conflict,[328] which the CRC Committee has recommended to set up,[329] in cooperation with national and international NGOs and UN bodies, such as UNICEF.[330] The programmes need to ensure the privacy of

---

[321] *Ibid.*

[322] CRC Committee, *Concluding Observations:* Sri Lanka (UN Doc. CRC/C/Add. 207, 2003), para. 45; Myanmar (UN Doc. CRC/C/Add. 237, 2004), para. 67(f).

[323] *Cf.* reporting guidelines for Article 6(3) (note 276).

[324] *Ibid.*

[325] Reporting guidelines for Article 6(3) (note 276).

[326] *Cf.* CRC Committee, *Concluding Observations:* India (UN Doc. CRC/C/Add. 228, 2004), para. 69.

[327] CRC Committee, *Concluding Observations:* Cambodia (UN Doc. CRC/C/Add. 128, 2000), para. 59; Colombia (UN Doc. CRC/C/Add. 137, 2000), para. 56. *Cf.* also CRC Committee, *Concluding Observations:* Indonesia (UN Doc. CRC/C/Add. 223, 2004), para. 72; Myanmar (UN Doc. CRC/C/Add. 237, 2004), para. 67(f).

[328] This also contributes to reintegration since child soldiers do not get isolated in these circumstances.

[329] CRC Committee, *Concluding Observations:* Sierra Leone (UN Doc. CRC/C/Add. 116, 2000), para. 74; Djibouti (UN Doc. CRC/C/Add. 131, 2000), para. 52; Colombia (UN Doc. CRC/C/Add. 137, 2000), para. 57; South Africa (UN Doc. CRC/C/Add. 122, 2000), para. 36; Sri Lanka (UN Doc. CRC/C/Add. 207, 2003), para. 45(b); Pakistan (UN Doc. CRC/C/Add. 217, 2003), para. 68; Papua New Guinea (UN Doc. CRC/C/Add. 229, 2004), para. 56; Indonesia (UN Doc. CRC/C/Add. 223, 2004), para. 72; Liberia (UN Doc. CRC/C/Add. 236, 2004), para. 59(c); Myanmar (UN Doc. CRC/C/Add. 237, 2004), para. 67(e). The UN also recommends that reintegration programmes should be comprehensive and should include specific provisions for child soldiers (United Nations Department of Peacekeeping Operations, *o.c.* (note 285), No 6).

[330] CRC Committee, *Concluding Observations:* Sierra Leone (UN Doc. CRC/C/Add. 116, 2000),

the children.[331] National institutions dealing with the release and/or recovery and reintegration of children should, according to the Committee, be allocated sufficient human and financial resources[332] to effectively demobilize and reintegrate children in society and to provide the necessary follow up.[333]

83. This assistance shall only be accorded 'when necessary'. Hence, States Parties are under an absolute but conditional obligation. It is unclear how it should be determined that assistance is necessary. Moreover, it is rightly observed that 'practice has shown that very few children come physically or psychologically undamaged out of an armed conflict in which they fought'.[334]

7. Article 7: International Cooperation

84. Article 7 of the Optional Protocol[335] concerns implementation through international cooperation. A first paragraph deals with interstate cooperation and a second paragraph discusses different ways of realizing this cooperation. The CRC itself does not contain a provision similar to Article 7.

---

para. 74; Cambodia (UN Doc. CRC/C/Add. 128, 2000), para. 59; Colombia (UN Doc. CRC/C/Add. 137, 2000), para. 57; Comores (UN Doc. CRC/C/Add. 141, 2000), para. 46; Guinea-Bissau (UN Doc. CRC/C/Add. 177, 2002), para. 49; Solomon Islands (UN Doc. CRC/C/Add. 208, 2003), para. 51; Sri Lanka (UN Doc. CRC/C/Add. 207, 2003), para. 45.

[331] CRC Committee, *Concluding Observations*: Sri Lanka (UN Doc. CRC/C/Add. 207, 02/07/2003, para. 45; Indonesia (UN Doc. CRC/C/Add. 223, 2004), para. 72; Myanmar (UN Doc. CRC/C/Add. 237, 2004), para. 67(e).

[332] *Cf.* CRC Committee, *Concluding Observations*: Chad (UN Doc. CRC/C/Add. 107, 1999), para. 35; Guatemala (UN Doc. CRC/C/Add. 154, 2001), para. 49 (National Commission for Searching for Disappeared Children); Democratic Republic of the Congo (UN Doc. CRC/C/Add. 153, 2001), para. 65 (DUNABER: special bureau for the demobilisation and reintegration of child soldiers).

[333] *Cf.* CRC Committee, *Concluding Observations*: Democratic Republic of the Congo (UN Doc. CRC/C/Add. 153, 2001), para. 65.

[334] J. Mermet, 'Protocole facultatif à la Convention relative aux droits de l'enfant concernant l'implication d'enfants dans les conflits armés: quel progrès pour la protection des droits de l'enfant?', *l.c.* (note 12), p. 4.

[335] The reporting guidelines for Article 7 determine:
'Reports should provide information on cooperation in the implementation of the Optional Protocol, including through technical cooperation and financial assistance. In this regard, reports should provide information, *inter alia*, on the extent of the technical cooperation or financial assistance, which the State Party has requested or offered. Please indicate, if the State Party is in a position of providing financial assistance, the existing multilateral, bilateral or other programmes that have been undertaken for that assistance.'

7.1   Article 7(1): Cooperation in the Implementation of the Protocol

85. According to Article 7(1), States Parties shall cooperate in the implementation of the Protocol, including in the prevention of any activity contrary thereto and in the rehabilitation and social reintegration of persons who are victims of acts contrary thereto, including through technical cooperation and financial assistance. Such assistance and cooperation will be undertaken in consultation with the States Parties concerned and the relevant international organizations.

The obligation to cooperate is an absolute obligation of result. It includes all aspects of the implementation of the Protocol, from prevention to rehabilitation and reintegration. States will for example have to cooperate in preventing and ending the use of under-18s by rebel groups. This is particularly relevant for States supporting or influencing these groups.[336]

Cooperation can take place by any means. Technical cooperation and financial assistance are two examples of such means. Consultation of the States Parties concerned and the relevant international organizations such as UNICEF,[337] the WHO,[338] etc.[339] is essential. The Optional Protocol thus seems to be departing from a positive obligation to cooperate or assist. From the concluding observations relating to the CRC as well as from the reporting guidelines,[340] it could also be derived that States Parties are under an obligation to actively seek for assistance from States Parties or international organizations.[341] In this regard, mention can be made of the recommendations to 'take all appropriate measures, *including through international cooperation*, if necessary'[342] and to 'redouble efforts to *allocate* the necessary

---

[336] M. Dennis, 'The ILO Convention on the worst forms of child labor', *l.c.* (note 142), p. 793.

[337] *Cf.* CRC Committee, *Concluding Observations*: Myanmar (UN Doc. CRC/C/Add. 237, 2004), para. 67(g).

[338] *Cf.* CRC Committee, *Concluding Observations*: Rwanda (UN Doc. CRC/C/Add. 234, 2004), para. 63(c).

[339] UNDP, UNHCR, UNCHS (Habitat) (CRC Committee, *Concluding Observations*: Guatemala (UN Doc. CRC/C/Add. 154, 2001), para. 49) and OHCHR (CRC Committee, *Concluding Observations*: Solomon Islands (UN Doc. CRC/C/Add. 208, 2003), para. 51(d)) could also be mentioned.

[340] '[...] reports should provide information, [...], on the extent of the technical cooperation or financial assistance which the State Party has *requested or offered*', emphasis added.

[341] *Cf.* also CRC Committee, *Concluding Observations*: Myanmar (UN Doc. CRC/C/Add. 69, 1997), para. 45; Yemen (UN Doc. CRC/C/Add. 102, 1999), para. 31; Georgia (UN Doc. CRC/C/Add. 124, 2000), para. 59; Ethiopia (UN Doc. CRC/C/Add. 144, 2001), para. 69.

[342] CRC Committee, *Concluding Observations*: Azerbaijan (UN Doc. CRC/C/Add. 77, 1997), para. 48, emphasis added.

resources, *if necessary with international assistance'*.[343] Some States were recently recommended to seek technical assistance from international organisations, such as UNICEF and the WHO.[344]

7.2   *Article 7(2): Programmes or Fund*

86. Article 7(2) determines that States Parties in a position to do so shall provide such assistance through existing multilateral, bilateral or other programmes or, *inter alia*, through a voluntary fund established in accordance with the rules of the General Assembly.

'Such assistance' refers to the financial assistance mentioned in Article 7(1). This view is supported by the reporting guidelines stating that 'if a State Party is in a position of providing financial assistance, it should indicate (. . .)'.[345] In other words, States Parties which have sufficient resources[346] are under an absolute obligation to financially assist under the form described in Article 7(2), i.e. through international programmes, which should preferably plan for long-term assistance,[347] and voluntary fund. It remains uncertain how it is to be determined which States have the financial means to assist in this way.

8.   *Article 8: Reporting*

87. In three paragraphs, Article 8 of the Optional Protocol deals with the modalities of the reporting procedure under the Optional Protocol. The Committee on the Rights of the Child, established by Article 43 CRC, is charged with the monitoring of the implementation of the Protocol through the examination of State reports.[348] The CRC Committee has developed comprehensive guidelines for the preparation of these reports.[349] The report-

---

[343] CRC Committee, *Concluding Observations:* Chad (UN Doc. CRC/C/Add. 107, 1999), para. 35, emphasis added.

[344] CRC Committee, *Concluding Observations:* Guinea-Bissau (UN Doc. CRC/C/Add. 177, 2002), para. 49(d); Solomon Islands (UN Doc. CRC/C/Add. 208, 2003), para. 51(d); Sri Lanka (UN Doc. CRC/C/Add. 207, 2003), para. 45(d); Myanmar (UN Doc. CRC/C/Add. 237, 2004), para. 67(g); Rwanda (UN Doc. CRC/C/Add. 234, 2004), para. 63(c).

[345] Reporting guidelines for Article 7 (note 337).

[346] Unicef, Guide, *o.c.* (note 54), p. 42.

[347] Security Council Resolution S/2000/101, 11 February 2000, The Role of United Nations Peacekeeping in Disarmament, Demobilisation and Reintegration, No 92.

[348] On the reporting procedure before the CRC Committee, see M. Verheyde and G. Goedertier, 'Articles 43-45: The Committee on the Rights of the Child', in: A. Alen, J. Ofde Lanotte, E. Verhellen, F. Ang, E. Berghmans and M. Verheyde (eds.), *A Commentary on the United Nations Convention on the Rights of the Child* (Leiden/Boston, Martinus Nijhoff Publishers, 2005), 50p.

[349] The reporting guidelines are not legally binding, but they are good indications of what the CRC Committee is expecting from States.

ing guidelines contain general directions and specific requirements per article of the Protocol. The latter have been discussed above. Under this heading, the general directions are dealt with.[350]

The first (and to date only) report under the Optional Protocol submitted to the Committee on the Rights of the Child was the report of New Zealand. After discussions with, *inter alia*, the government representatives, the Committee issued its concluding observations.[351] These have, when relevant, been examined above. It is interesting to note that the CRC Committee regretted the fact that the delegation did not include a member of the Ministry of Defence to answer specific questions.[352] Other countries could thus consider the inclusion of a member of this ministry (or another institution having similar tasks) in their delegations.

8.1 Article 8(1): Initial Reports

88. Article 8(1) concerns the initial reports. States Parties shall, within two years following the entry into force of the Protocol for that State, submit a report to the Committee on the Rights of the Child providing comprehensive information on the measures it has taken to implement the provisions of the Protocol, including the measures taken to implement the provisions on participation and recruitment. As was already mentioned, the Committee on the Rights of the Child is thus the monitoring mechanism of the Optional Protocol.

---

[350] Pursuant to the introductory party of the guidelines:
'Reports should provide information on the measures adopted by the State Party to give effect to the rights set forth in the Optional Protocol and on the progress made in the enjoyment of those rights and should indicate the factors and difficulties, if any, affecting the degree of fulfilment of the obligations under the Optional Protocol.

Copies of the principal legislative texts and judicial decisions, administrative bodies and other relevant instructions to the armed forces, both of a civil and military character, as well as detailed statistical information, indicators referred therein and relevant research should accompany reports. In reporting to the Committee, States Parties should indicate how the implementation of the Optional Protocol is in line with the general principles of the Convention on the Rights of the Child, namely non-discrimination, best interests of the child, right to life, survival and development, and respect for the views of the child. Moreover, the process of preparation of the report should be described to the Committee, including the involvement of governmental and non-governmental organizations/bodies in its drafting and dissemination. Finally, reports should indicate the date of reference used when determining whether or not a person is within an age limit (for instance, the date of birth of the person concerned or the first day of the year during which the person concerned reaches that age limit).'

[351] The report of New Zealand on the Optional Protocol to the Convention on the Rights of the Child was discussed together with the country's report on the Convention in the Committee's 34th session in September 2003.

[352] CRC Committee, *Concluding Observations*: New Zealand (UN Doc. CRC/C/OPAC/CO/2003/NZL, 2003), introduction.

States Parties are under an obligation of result to submit their first report within two years following the entry into force of the Protocol for that State Party (*Cf. infra* No 99), i.e. two years and one month after ratification or accession. A similar reporting obligation can be found in Article 44 of the CRC. However, this obligation seems weaker than the one under the Protocol, since it determines that States 'undertake to submit' a report. A reporting procedure has its weaknesses. A common problem under the CRC is the fact that most States do not meet the deadlines for submitting their reports.[353] To date, this is also the case with reports due under the Protocol.[354] It remains to be awaited what consequences this could have, given the fact that the obligation pursuant to Article 8(1) is absolute. Possibly, the introduction of an obligation of result is only a means of pressure without direct implications.

In their reports, States must provide comprehensive information on the measures taken to implement the Protocol, including to implement the provisions on participation and recruitment. The reporting guidelines contain more detailed indications on the general content of this comprehensive report. Copies of the principal legislation, judicial decisions and administrative and other relevant instructions to the armed forces, both civilly and militarily, need to accompany the report. Detailed statistical information, indicators referred therein and relevant research should be provided as well.[355]

The information asked for in the reporting guidelines implies that an evaluation of the progress in the enjoyment of the rights under the Optional Protocol is to be made, whereby the factors and difficulties affecting the fulfilment of those rights should be indicated. This guideline is inspired by Article 44(2) of the CRC. States should thus 'assess the effect of the measures they took and (. . .) check whether those have contributed to the realisation of the rights of the child'.[356]

---

[353] *Cf.* G. Goedertier and M. Verheyde, 'The Activities of the UN Committee on the Rights of the Child', in: E. Verhellen (ed.), *Understanding Children's Rights*, (Ghent, University of Ghent: Children's Rights centre, 2001), p. 396.

[354] On 1 September 2004, 36 country reports were overdue, namely the reports of Andorra, Austria, Azerbaijan, Bangladesh, Belgium, Bulgaria, Canada, Cape Verde, Czech Republic, Democratic Republic of the Congo, El Salvador, Guatemala, Holy See, Iceland, Italy, Jamaica, Kenya, Mali, Malta, Mexico, Monaco, Morocco, Namibia, Panama, Peru, Philippines, Qatar, Romania, Rwanda, Sierra Leone, Spain, Sri Lanka, Switzerland, Uganda, Venezuela, Viet Nam.

[355] Reporting guidelines, introduction.

[356] G. Goedertier and M. Verheyde, 'The Activities of the UN Committee on the Rights of the Child', *l.c.* (note 354), p. 382.

States Parties should also evaluate the extent to which the implementation of the Optional Protocol is in line with the general principles of the CRC.[357] Hence, the Committee considers not only compliance with each article of the Optional Protocol but also adherence to the Convention's general principles, namely non-discrimination, best interests of the child, right to life, survival and development, and respect for the views of the child.[358]

The process of preparation of the report is also important. States should describe it to the Committee, thereby mentioning the governmental and non-governmental organizations or bodies involved in its drafting and dissemination.[359] The involvement of as many different actors as possible contributes to the accuracy and reliability of the report.

8.2   Article 8(2): Periodic Reporting

90. Article 8(2) states that, following the submission of the comprehensive report, each State Party shall include in the reports it submits to the Committee on the Rights of the Child, in accordance with Article 44 of the CRC, any further information with respect to the implementation of the Protocol. Other States Parties to the Protocol shall submit a report every five years. Hence, States must periodically report on the implementation of the Protocol. In a rather unclear wording, Article 8(2) distinguishes between States that are Party to the CRC and States that are not Party to this Convention. Both can become party to the Protocol (*Cf. infra* No 97).

8.2.1   States Parties to the Convention on the Rights of the Child
91. Since only States Parties to the Convention on the Rights of the Child can provide reports following Article 44 of the CRC, it is clear that the first sentence of Article 8(2) refers to these States. According to the mentioned Article 44, periodic reports are to be submitted every five years. For States Parties to the Optional Protocol, these shall include 'any further information with respect to the implementation of the Protocol'. It is unclear how this obligation of result should be interpreted. In a narrow interpretation, the phrase might be seen as 'encompassing only further governmental measures, rather than the continued implementation of measures already reported to the CRC Committee in the initial reports'.[360] It is to be hoped

---

[357] Reporting guidelines, introduction.
[358] Unicef, Guide, *o.c.* (note 54), p. 36.
[359] Reporting guidelines, introduction.
[360] M. Happold, 'The Optional Protocol to the Convention on the Rights of the Child on the involvement of children in armed conflict', *l.c.* (note 32), p. 240.

however that the Committee will interpret the provision broadly.[361] Indeed, monitoring mechanisms function best when as much relevant information as possible is at the disposition of the monitoring body.

8.2.2 *Other States Parties*

92. The second sentence of Article 8(2) refers to 'other States Parties', i.e. States that are not party to the CRC.[362] They are under an obligation of result to submit a periodic report every five years. The content of this report has not been precised.

8.3   *Article 8(3): Request for Further Information*

93. Pursuant to Article 8(3), the Committee on the Rights of the Child may request from States Parties further information relevant to the implementation of the Protocol. This article is similar to Article 44(4) of the CRC. Although the CRC Committee can request additional information from States, Article 8(3) does not impose on States the obligation to actually provide this information. Moreover, it is unclear what needs to be understood by 'further information relevant to the implementation of the Protocol'.

94. It should be noted that the Committee also welcomes information on the implementation of the CRC from other sources, including civil society and NGOs, UN agencies, other intergovernmental organizations and academic institutions. They can provide parallel or 'shadow' reports.[363]

9. *Article 9: Signature, Ratification/Accession*

95. Since the Optional Protocol establishes rights and obligations additional to those established by the CRC, the Protocol is considered to be independent from the Convention and must thus be ratified or acceded to in a separate process.[364] This process is dealt with in Article 9.

96. According to Article 9(1), the Optional Protocol is open for signature by any State that is a Party to the CRC or has signed it. The signature of the Protocol does not create a binding legal obligation, nor does it commit a

---

[361] *Ibid.*
[362] To date, this is only the case for the USA and Somalia.
[363] Unicef, Guide, *o.c.* (note 54), p. 37.
[364] Unicef, Guide, *o.c.* (note 54), p. 21.

State to proceed to ratification.[365] However, it creates an obligation to refrain from acts which would defeat the object and purpose of the Protocol.[366] For example, a State having signed the Protocol should not pass legislation lowering the age for voluntary recruitment.[367] In the absence of an express prohibition, signature is possible at any time.[368]

The only two States that are not party to the CRC are Somalia and the United States. Since they both signed the Convention,[369] they are also allowed to sign the Protocol.

97. Article 9(2) determines that the Protocol is subject to ratification and is open to accession by any State. Instruments of ratification or accession shall be deposited with the Secretary-General of the United Nations.

Any State can ratify or accede to the Protocol. States that are not party to the CRC, can thus become Party to the Optional Protocol. This is highly unusual: most optional protocols are open to ratification only by States Parties to the underlying treaty.[370] The provision was adopted under pressure of the United States.[371]

Ratification and accession both have the same legal effects, implying that a State definitively consents to be bound by the Protocol.[372] Whereas in case of ratification[373] a State first signs and then ratifies the Protocol, there is no signature prior to accession.[374,375] Although it is not mandatory for States to adopt all legislative and other measures outlined by the Optional Protocol

---

[365] M. Nowak, o.c. (note 3), p. 631, No 1; Unicef, Guide, o.c. (note 54), p. 22.

[366] Article 18 of the VCLT; Cf. Nowak, o.c. (note 3), p. 631, No 1.

[367] Unicef, Guide, o.c. (note 54), p. 22.

[368] M. Nowak, o.c. (note 3), p. 631, No 1.

[369] According to Article 46 of the CRC, the Convention is open for signature by any State. Somalia signed on 9 May 2002 and the USA on 16 February 1995.

[370] Unicef, Guide, o.c. (note 54), p. 21. J. Mermet observes that the text of this Article sets a bad precedent in international law (J. Mermet, 'Protocole facultatif à la Convention relative aux droits de l'enfant concernant l'implication d'enfants dans les conflits armés: quel progrès pour la protection des droits de l'enfant?', l.c. (note 12), p. 6.

[371] Cf. M. Happold, 'The Optional Protocol to the Convention on the Rights of the Child on the involvement of children in armed conflict', l.c. (note 32), p. 241. The USA became party to the Optional Protocol on 23 December 2002. The country still has not ratified the CRC although it signed this Convention.

[372] Cf. M. Nowak, o.c.(note 3), p. 631, No 2; Unicef, Guide, o.c. (note 54), p. 22.

[373] By ratification is meant the definitive consent to be bound by the treaty taking place in official form, usually by the Head of State. In a democratic State, ratification is generally preceded by parliamentary approval (M. Nowak, o.c. (note 3), p. 631, No 2.

[374] Accession replaces signature and ratification and ensues like the latter by deposit of a corresponding instrument with the Secretary-General (M. Nowak, o.c. (note 3), p. 632, No 3).

[375] Unicef, Guide, o.c. (note 54), p. 22.

prior to ratification or accession, they are nevertheless expected to comply with their obligations within a reasonable time after they become Party.[376]

As is the case with all treaties negotiated under the auspices of the UN,[377] notably with the CRC,[378] the instruments of ratification or accession must be deposited with the Secretary-General. Pursuant to Article 3(2) of the Protocol, these instruments must be accompanied by a binding declaration setting forth the minimum age for voluntary recruitment and the minimum safeguards adopted in that regard (*Cf. supra* No 50). If not, the instrument of ratification or accession cannot be accepted.[379]

98. As states Article 9(3), the Secretary-General, in his capacity as depository of the Convention and the Protocol, shall inform all States Parties to the Convention and all States that have signed the Convention of each instrument of declaration pursuant to Article 3.

10. *Article 10: Entry into Force*

99. Article 10 deals with the entry into force of the Optional Protocol as such and for each State Party.

According to Article 10(1), the Protocol enters into force three months after the deposit of the tenth instrument of ratification or accession. This was the case on 12 February 2002.[380]

Article 10(2) determines that for each State ratifying the Protocol or acceding to it after its entry into force, the Protocol enters into force one month after the date of the deposit of its own instrument of ratification or accession. One month is a relatively short period of time. States thus need to take sufficient measures prior to and just after adherence, in order not to violate the provisions of the Optional Protocol immediately.[381]

---

[376] *Ibid.*

[377] M. Happold, 'The Optional Protocol to the Convention on the Rights of the Child on the involvement of children in armed conflict', *l.c.* (note 32), p. 241; M. Nowak, *o.c.* (note 3), p. 645, No 2; *Cf.* also Article 102(1) of the UN Charter and Article 80 of the VCLT.

[378] Articles 47, 48 and 53 of the CRC.

[379] Unicef, Guide, *o.c.* (note 54), p. 23.

[380] The first ten States to become Party to the Optional Protocol were the following: Andorra, Austria, Bangladesh, Canada, Democratic Republic of the Congo, Holy See, Iceland, New Zealand, Romania, Sri Lanka.

[381] M. Happold, 'The Optional Protocol to the Convention on the Rights of the Child on the involvement of children in armed conflict', *l.c.* (note 32), p. 241.

11. *Article 11: Denunciation*

100. States are not obliged to stay Party to the Protocol: they can denounce it. The procedure to do so is described in Article 11.

Article 11(1) states that any State Party may denounce the Protocol at any time by written notification to the Secretary-General of the United Nations, who shall thereafter inform the other States Parties to the Convention and all States that have signed the Convention. The denunciation takes effect one year after the date of receipt of the notification by the Secretary-General. If, however, on the expiry of that year the denouncing State Party is engaged in armed conflict, the denunciation shall not take effect before the end of the armed conflict. The last provision must assure that no State denounces the Protocol just because it wants to stop complying with its provisions immediately. As far as armed conflicts are concerned, no distinction is made between international and internal armed conflicts.[382] The CRC itself may also be denounced by written notification to the Secretary-General of the United Nations. This denunciation becomes effective one year after the date of receipt of the notification by the Secretary-General.[383]

According to Article 11(2), the denunciation shall not have the effect of releasing the State Party from its obligations under the Protocol in regard to any act that occurs prior to the date on which the denunciation becomes effective. The denunciation shall neither prejudice in any way the continued consideration of any matter that is already under consideration by the Committee on the Rights of the Child prior to the date on which the denunciation becomes effective. This provision must assure that no State denounces the Protocol to escape from the effects of non-compliance.

12. *Article 12: Amendments*

101. In three paragraphs, Article 12 describes the procedure to amend the Optional Protocol.

Pursuant to Article 12(1), any State Party may propose an amendment and file it with the Secretary-General of the United Nations. The Secretary-General shall thereupon communicate the proposed amendment to the States Parties. He will request them to indicate whether they favour a conference of States Parties for the purpose of considering and voting upon the

---

[382] *Ibid.*
[383] Article 52 of the CRC.

proposals. In the event that, within four months from the date of such communication, at least one third of the States Parties favour such a conference, the Secretary-General shall convene the conference under the auspices of the UN. Any amendment adopted by a majority of States Parties present and voting at the conference shall be submitted to the General Assembly of the UN for approval. The process of amendment is thus rather lengthy and complex,[384] but is the same as the procedure contained in Article 50(1) of the CRC, and is inspired by notably Article 51 of the 1966 ICCPR.

Article 12(2) determines that an amendment adopted in accordance with paragraph 1 will enter into force when it has been approved by the General Assembly and accepted by a two-third majority of States Parties. This is also the case under Article 50(2) of the CRC.

Article 12(3) states that an amendment entering into force shall be binding on those States Parties that have accepted it, other States still being bound by the provisions of the Protocol and any earlier amendments they have accepted. Article 50(3) contains the same provision. It is regretted that the Protocol does not permit the adoption of amendments binding on all States Parties by a majority vote.[385] This would for example allow the majority of States to impose a higher age limit for voluntary recruitment on all States.

13. Article 13: Authentic Versions, Deposit, Transmission of Copies

102. Article 13 deals with some practical matters.

According to Article 13(1), the Arabic, Chinese, English, French, Russian and Spanish texts are equally authentic. They shall be deposited in the archives of the United Nations. The text of the Protocol is thus equally authentic in all UN languages. This means that these six languages are equally controlling for the interpretation of the text.[386] Article 54 CRC contains the same provision.

Pursuant to Article 13(2), the Secretary-General of the UN shall transmit certified copies of the Protocol to all States Parties to the Convention and all States having signed the Convention.

---

[384] M. Happold, 'The Optional Protocol to the Convention on the Rights of the Child on the involvement of children in armed conflict', l.c. (note 32), p. 242; Cf. also M. Nowak, o.c. (note 3), p. 640, No 1 (concerning the ICCPR).

[385] M. Happold, 'The Optional Protocol to the Convention on the Rights of the Child on the involvement of children in armed conflict', l.c. (note 32), p. 242.

[386] Cf. Article 33 of the VCLT; M. Nowak, o.c. (note 3), p. 645, No 1.